D0769656

HAUNTED

ASYLUMS, PRISONS,
AND
SANATORIUMS

About Jamie Davis

I've always been interested in the paranormal and abandoned buildings. I have never seen a door I didn't long to open or a staircase I didn't desire to climb. It started when I was a kid, when I would check out every book I could find from the local library on ghosts and hauntings, and watch as many scary movies as possible. As early as the age of four, I remember being obsessed with old, abandoned homes.

Somewhere around 2009, I decided that I needed to start traveling more and soon after that, my paranormal adventures began. The road has taken me to many unexpected places, and I have enjoyed every second of it. I hope to always be a traveler, soaking up whatever the world has to offer me, knowing that the fun is in the journey itself. There are few answers to be had, few absolute truths in this life—such a temporary, fleeting thing. But still: seek and you will find. Keep searching. Sometimes you will find only what you want to find. Sometimes you will find what you didn't even know you were looking for. Either way is fine.

To Write to the Author

If you wish to contact the author or would like more information about this book, please write to the author in care of Llewellyn Worldwide, and we will forward your request. Both the author and the publisher appreciate hearing from you and learning of your enjoyment of this book and how it has helped you. Llewellyn Worldwide cannot guarantee that every letter written to the author can be answered, but all will be forwarded. Please write to:

Jamie Davis
⁒ Llewellyn Worldwide
2143 Wooddale Drive
Woodbury, MN 55125-2989

Please enclose a self-addressed stamped envelope for reply,
or $1.00 to cover costs. If outside the USA, enclose
an international postal reply coupon.

JAMIE DAVIS
WITH SAM QUEEN

HAUNTED
ASYLUMS, PRISONS,
AND
SANATORIUMS

INSIDE THE ABANDONED INSTITUTIONS FOR
THE CRAZY, CRIMINAL & QUARANTINED

Llewellyn Publications
Woodbury, Minnesota

FIRST EDITION
Second Printing, 2013

Book design by Bob Gaul
Cover photo © Jamie Davis
Cover design by Ellen Lawson
Editing by Ed Day
Interior photos by Samuel Queen and Jamie Davis

Llewellyn Publications is a registered trademark of Llewellyn Worldwide Ltd.

Library of Congress Cataloging-in-Publication Data
Davis, Jamie, 1981–
   Haunted asylums, prisons, and sanatoriums: inside the abandoned institutions for the crazy, criminal & quarantined/Jamie Davis with Sam Queen.— First edition
       pages cm
   Includes bibliographical references.
   ISBN 978-0-7387-3750-8
1. Haunted prisons—United States. 2. Asylums—United States. 3. Sanatoriums—United States. I. Queen, Sam. II. Title.
   BF1477.3.D38 2013
   133.1'22—dc23
                              2013010012

Llewellyn Worldwide Ltd. does not participate in, endorse, or have any authority or responsibility concerning private business transactions between our authors and the public.
   All mail addressed to the author is forwarded, but the publisher cannot, unless specifically instructed by the author, give out an address or phone number.
   Any Internet references contained in this work are current at publication time, but the publisher cannot guarantee that a specific location will continue to be maintained. Please refer to the publisher's website for links to authors' websites and other sources.

Llewellyn Publications
A Division of Llewellyn Worldwide Ltd.
2143 Wooddale Drive
Woodbury, MN 55125-2989
www.llewellyn.com

Printed in the United States of America

CONTENTS

ACKNOWLEDGMENTS

To my ghost hunting partner and best friend, Sam Queen. Without you this book would not have been possible. You are a tireless road warrior who has spent countless hours sitting in the dark listening to my musings/ramblings/mumblings and toting my bags through the airport. You spent your free time reviewing every piece of audio evidence we have ever collected and researching locations featured on *Diners, Drive-ins and Dives* to find us plenty of good places to eat while we were traveling! Thank you for having this adventure with me.

To Mom and Dad, for always encouraging my interests. You ingrained a sense of independence and confidence in me that will carry me through life. You taught me that I can do anything that I want, and I still maybe believe that, except for the being the president part. I'm pretty sure that's not going to happen. But I wouldn't rule it out.

To my sister Holly, brother-in-law Doug, and nephews Griffin and Tanner. Because who knows if I will ever write another book.

To Keri Jean—my favorite cousin and my heart—and her beautiful brood—husband Brian and three tow-headed babies: Parker, Cayden, and Ava Reese.

Aunt Carol, Uncle Bob, and Maw-Maw. Sure wish Paw-Paw could read this book!

To Amy Goldstone, my very best girl friend, who works side by side with me every day and who has provided endless encouragement to keep on keeping on with the project (even when I thought no one was going to sign these photo releases)!

And to DWP, JRH, RCF, JDM, SGL, and MEM (my trial lawyers), and all the HPLiens at the firm—thank you for encouraging my interests, both personal hobbies and law related, and for just generally being great people to work for and with. I am very lucky to have all of you.

Joel Hiscutt—our very first tour guide who led us through a dark asylum in western New York and who first showed us the flashlight experiment that blew our minds. Joel, you pretty much helped inspire our curiosity about ghost hunting. Thank you.

To the owners and staff of these places, who preserve history and provide a safe place for people to come in and explore and investigate.

To countless other family members, friends, and associates.

To the strangers sitting and waiting next to us in airports and on airplanes, who struck up conversations to pass the time, and then became genuinely intrigued by our project. Random strangers in every city we went to provided encouragement and critiques along the way. My travels have taught me that EVERYONE likes a good ghost story —and most likely has one of their own to share.

Visit *www.facebook.com/pages/Haunted-Asylums-Prisons-and-Sanatoriums /539590409393229* to view all of the color photos taken at each location, listen to EVPs, and watch the flashlight videos for yourself!

A Note from
the Contributing Author

First off, let me say that I am a Christian. I believe in life after death. I have a strong faith in this, but what are ghosts, exactly? I don't think that we will ever find answers as to what ghosts are, at least not while we're living and breathing here on earth. Until recently, I never really thought that ghosts and hauntings were real. I thought that there may be a possibility of the paranormal but pretty much just chalked it up to legends, myths, Hollywood magic, and the like. Regarding ghosts, to me "seeing is believing." During this past year, I have seen and I believe.

My brother, Stewart, called me one day and told me that there was this new reality show coming to television. It was called *Ghost Hunters*. I became a fan from the first episode. I like the way that they try to disprove reports instead of saying every sound and shadow are paranormal. After watching this show, I started to come around to the idea that ghosts are real. But still, this is a television show. It's entertainment.

How do you know what they're doing is really legit? You don't really know unless you experience these things for yourself, which is what Jamie and I did.

I want to thank my best friend, Jamie Davis. This has been a wonderful journey. It's something that I never will forget! Thanks also for the support of my family and friends, and to Jamie's father and brother-in-law for helping get us to where we wanted to go.

Visit *www.facebook.com/pages/Haunted-Asylums-Prisons-and-Sanatoriums /539590409393229* to view all of the color photos taken at each location, listen to EVPs, and watch the flashlight videos for yourself!

INTRODUCTION

Sam and I spent our 2009 and 2010 summer vacations in Estes Park, Colorado, hiking the Rocky Mountains and staying at the famous Stanley Hotel (the inspiration for Stephen King's *The Shining*). We are fans of the TV shows *Ghost Hunters* and *Ghost Adventures* and had first heard of the hotel through a special episode of *Ghost Hunters*. We were strictly traveling as tourists, though, not ghost hunters. We took the ghost tour offered by the hotel, and it was fun, but we never spent any serious time trying to investigate the place on our own. Well, I say that. There was one small incident that occurred in room 418. We were in for the night and sitting in the dark trying to communicate with a spirit. Sam said, "Feel free to touch me or knock on the wall," and I said, "Don't touch me!" He is always saying stuff like that, and I hate it! I don't want somebody touching me—alive, dead, in between, whatever! Don't touch me. Anyway, we went to bed with the camera on the nightstand, and when we woke up, it was perfectly placed (sitting upright) under the middle of the bed. That certainly got us scratching our heads! There was no way that camera could have fallen off the nightstand and rolled itself into an upright position! We could not duplicate the effect. Also that night, we heard people walking around above us (even though there was no floor above us)! I dismissed it and tried to go to sleep.

In April 2010, while planning a trip to New York, I saw an old *Ghost Adventures* episode where they were investigating an asylum in western New York. I wondered aloud how far the asylum was from where we were staying and found a website for the asylum that indicated that they were offering public ghost hunts the weekend we would be there. I floated the idea with Sam before I purchased the tickets. We both thought it would be a really unique, interesting side trip from the normal touristy type things. It had never occurred to us (even after seven years of watching paranormal shows!) that anyone could actually visit some of these places! You don't have to have any special equipment or belong to any organization. You just buy a ticket and show up.

Our trip to the asylum was phenomenal. It made me want to try to develop the sensitivities that I first demonstrated at the age of four. (At the age of four, my Uncle Paul died. He was the youngest of the Sanford children—in his early twenties and still living with my grandparents at the time. The first Christmas without him, my father caught me staring up at the balcony. Although I don't remember it, I am told that I was staring because Paul was leaning on the railing watching us open our presents. My father saw him, too.) After our very first visit to the asylum, we were hooked into the field, and I was inspired to write this book. I came home and scoured the Internet looking for a guide book to other famous haunted locations that offered public ghost hunts. I couldn't find one, so I made up my mind to write one myself.

Ghost hunting is one of the biggest thrill-seeking activities that I have ever participated in. Nothing provides the same adrenaline rush. You are alone in the dark. You hear something or think you see something. What do you do? Stick around and try to figure out the logical explanation? Or run towards the nearest exit? It is a wonderful psychological experiment just to see where your own fear takes your mind in this situation. And once you start seeing the lights on the K2 meter go from green to red, or flashlights light up in response to your questions, you're hooked.

Of course, I have my other personal reasons for doing it—you wouldn't do it if you didn't have that most basic initial desire to figure out whether there is something else out there. A sort of gut feeling that we are not alone in the world and a natural curiosity to explore what else—who else—is sharing our world. I know you're not supposed to admit this, but if you deny doing it for the fun of it, then you're lying. The cold hard truth of it is that if it wasn't exciting or fun, you would go do something else. You could conduct your research from a warm, cozy library or settle in your office with a big cup of coffee and read about ghost hunting on the Internet. The fact that it is interesting, thrilling, and fun is in no way disrespectful to any spirit. The evidence we have collected supports that, and it really will speak for itself.

There are places across the country that offer the same type of private and public ghost hunts that the asylum in western New York does. All of the locations are fascinating, steeped in history, and interesting to visit in the light of day. Many of them offer historical tours, which I would encourage you to take. In fact, I would say that it is absolutely necessary to see the location during the day. Not only will it help you acclimate yourself to the building, it will also leave you with different impressions than you can get at night. After the sun goes down, these places open their doors to seasoned ghost hunters, novices, or paranormal enthusiasts/tourists. They provide a safe environment for people to come in and investigate. You can go in on a public hunt or take a team up and book a private event. You can investigate some of the most reportedly haunted locations in this country and decide for yourself: Is this place just hype, or is there something more to it than just legends and stories?

Whether you are a seasoned investigator who has every one of these locations on your list of places to visit or if you are just curious about the field, this book is for you. This is not a book about how to ghost hunt. This is simply our report of what it was like for us to ghost hunt at famous locations (a travel guide of sorts) and what happened to us along the way.

I will say that when we first started this project, I had several preconceived notions. One of them was that spirits were somehow confined to the buildings we were in and never went anywhere else. We also had the idea that when you died, you either immediately went to heaven or hell, and that all of these ghosts out here had to be lost souls who were stuck on earth. I surmised that ghosts had to be either confused over their own death (not realizing they were dead) or fixated on some type of unfinished business. I also thought that nighttime would logically be the best time to investigate any paranormal activity. To say the least, these ideas have changed based on our experiences. And we have changed from our experiences. For instance, I discovered that I think I might be an empath. An empath is a person who can pick up on the emotions of others. I found that as time went on, I became more sensitive to "feeling" the energy in a place. It was a part of my brain that was developing. Just like exercising a muscle to get it toned up, the same idea rings true. We are still floored by the amount of intelligent, responsive, and even humorous activity that we encountered!

Equipment/Processes Used

I wanted to learn more about the paranormal field and develop my natural, God-given abilities using all of my senses and intuitiveness. The best way I could think of to educate myself was to actually visit some of the most famous locations in the country and use them as a sort of training ground. So while we did have fun on our adventures, we were also very much attending school, paying attention, and studying. Due to time and budget constraints, we were only able to visit each location once. Believe me, I wish we could have experienced each location multiple times. Hopefully we will be able to do so in the future.

Since the goal for me was to develop my own senses, we did not rely on a truckload of equipment. All of the so-called science behind ghost hunting is speculative anyway, so we didn't want to get too bogged down with expensive equipment on our first run out.

We kept it simple—notepads and pens, a digital voice recorder (we do not have any fancy or expensive software to clean up the background noise), three twist-top flashlights, a K2 meter, and an IR camera.

Ghost Augustine, a ghost tour and equipment company, explains the ranges of measurement that pertain to the K2 as follows:

- The K2 EMF meter measures EMF strengths in the scale of milligauss.

- 1st light (GREEN) indicates a normal background EMF field which we always have around us between 0 and 1.5 mG.

- 2nd light (GREEN) indicates a low-level EMF between 1.5 and 2.5 mG.

- 3rd light (YELLOW) indicates a mid-level EMF in the range between 2.5 and 10 mG.

- 4th light (ORANGE) indicates a high-level EMF field in the range between 10 and 20 mG.

- 5th Light (RED) indicates an extremely high EMF of more than 20 mG.

Okay. Well, what is that supposed to mean to me, and how do you use the meter? The theory is that ghosts or spirits give off some kind of magnetic energy that can be detected by this meter after you eliminate any man-made fields in the area. The first step is to take a sweep of the room you are investigating to identify any man-made spikes of EMF. For example, if you sweep it close to your microwave or any electronics in your living room, you should see some kind of a spike on the meter.

(Mine will light up to the midway/yellow point around the microwave.) What you are trying to do is establish a baseline in the room and note where you are getting hits on the meter before you even start your paranormal investigation. One point to note is that rooms with high EMF readings have been known to produce effects that mimic paranormal claims, such as feelings of nausea, dizziness, headache, fatigue, weakness, and altered perceptions. Quite simply, you didn't see a ghost; the high EMF is just messing with your brain. Is the meter a ghost detector? I don't know. But it is interesting when you've cleared a room by walking around it slowly with the meter at arm's length and your baseline is green the entire time, and then suddenly you ask a question and the meter lights up like crazy all the way to red!

The digital voice recorder is used to try to capture EVPs (electronic voice phenomena). Skeptics will say that what you are experiencing is radio interference or that the supposed voice you hear is just a form of auditory pareidolia—and that your brain is just doing its job to attempt to make some sense out of nonsensical noise. They will say that if you want to hear something badly enough, you will. But I think some of these noises (or voices) are actually pretty compelling pieces of evidence. Why can't you hear it with your ears at the time? What is it about the recorder that allows you to hear these spirit voices? My personal mundane explanation is that humans simply cannot hear sounds on every frequency. The low frequencies are called infrasound, which I think of as the same way you listen for a heartbeat. High frequencies are known as ultrasound, and an example of this would be how dolphins communicate. If you're interested in more details, you can find countless scientific journals and articles on the Internet that explain how humans process sound, how frequency is measured in hertz, and the like.

My very favorite paranormal experiment to conduct is to use the flashlights to communicate (nothing like a little instant gratification), even though it invites criticism. Anyone who has never tried this will tear it to pieces, and I fully expect that the world will tear apart all of the videos that we have captured. I don't care. I know what happened to us, and I know that it was real. Try it yourself before you criticize it. I can assure you we didn't somehow figure out how to rig those lights and manipulate them with some sort of magic button. Anyone who knows us will tell you we aren't smart enough to put the fix on the flashlights. There is no trick to it. We twisted the screw-tops just a bit to make them easier to manipulate, and we laid them on the ground. Sometimes they are responsive, sometimes they're not. We have hours of video where they never light up and hours of video where it seems like we are talking to someone. I hear that this is very rare—especially considering the short amount of time we spent in each location. The flashlights have rolled around my car for three hours at a time and never lit up. I've stomped right next to them to see if that motion will do anything to turn the flashlights on. The movement doesn't turn the lights on. I don't know HOW it works exactly, except to say that something—some ghost or spirit—is able to draw energy from it and communicate that way. It is very real to me while it is happening. And it is still real to me after going back and watching the videos. In the beginning, it would take up to three hours to get any sort of flashlight activity to happen. As time went on and we kept traveling, it seemed as though we were having things happen to us within the first twenty minutes of sitting down talking, sometimes even quicker than that! This intrigues me. Did we get better at communicating with spirits? Did we just get lucky in capturing these videos? I am almost inclined to think that we just got better at clearing our minds, concentrating, and listening, although I have never been one to underestimate the luck of being at the right place at the right time!

Our approach to ghost hunting has worked for us. It's the result of time constraints and personality. I have no patience—for ghost hunting or waiting for anything in general. I like to get a task completed in the best and most efficient way possible. I'll say, "I'm Jamie, and this is Sam. We're from Atlanta, and we've traveled a long way. I'm tired. We're only here for a short time, so if someone has something to say, now's the time to do it, because I need to be asleep by 1:00 a.m." It has seemed to work extremely well for us. Why should I have to go sit somewhere for days on end in order to capture evidence? Quite frankly, I don't have that kind of time. And unless you are getting paid to investigate for a living, I don't imagine anyone would have that kind of time. However, it does make me wonder what kind of evidence I would turn up if I could go sit somewhere for days on end like the pros do.

There have been many occasions where I have flat out begged for something to occur, and I believe that has worked in some instances. My pleas were heard. No one has time to waste—not us, not them. And to think that something or someone is just sitting in a dark room waiting for you to come along and grace them with your presence in order to have a deep conversation about whether or not they are male or female, adult or child, well, I would say that you're mistaken.

For every place we entered, the first thing we said was, "We're just here to talk to anyone who wants to talk to us. We don't want to bother anybody, and we don't want anybody to bother us." We had conversations the same way we would talk to anyone. The only difference is we just couldn't hear anyone talking back to us (until we got home and listened to the voice recorder). When we were done, we thanked the person for their time. And when we were packing up the car and preparing to drive away, we said, "If anyone is with us, you can't come home with us. You have to leave." Except for that one time we forgot at Yorktown. And then I had something follow me home.

Sam saw an apparition at St. Albans and shadow people at Waverly Hills. I saw a shadow person at the Farrar School, and we both saw the same shadow person at the same time at Missouri State Penitentiary! This journey has changed us. For the better, I think. We've learned and grown from our travels. One small example of that is that in the beginning, I could not walk into a dark room by myself. Fear just took hold of me and paralyzed me. Like any good students, we know that our studying is never over. We don't know anything for certain (and realize that we never will), except that there is something else out there besides us.

But we knew that before we even began. We just didn't have any video or recorded evidence of it yet.

Sam and I set off on our journey with absolutely no clue of what we were going to experience. We just wanted some excitement in our lives, and maybe a little fun and adventure. There was no way that either one of us could have foreseen what was to come. We were determined to visit some of the most allegedly haunted places in America and report on our experiences.

ONE

ASHMORE ESTATES —
ASHMORE, ILLINOIS

The Coles County Almshouse (or Poor Farm) was created in 1857. The residents ranged from alcoholics and misdemeanor criminals to people with mental disabilities, orphans, widows, and the elderly. They were given chores to do, grew their own food, and kept animals. These were people who had no place else to live. Maybe for some it was a place of refuge, but it appears to me to have been a place where people just ended up. A place for social outcasts and people who the world had forgotten about or wanted to forget.

Ashmore Estates.

In 1902, the Board of State Commissioners completed this report on the farm:

Coles

The sanitary condition of this building is fair. The heating is by stoves and is sufficient. There is no regular system of ventilation, but plenty of fresh air is easily obtained. There is no plumbing. The water supply is from a well and cistern. There is no fire protection.

There is no special provision for the insane. One inmate who is insane has not been so adjudged by the court. None are locked up or in restraint. There is one inmate who never has outdoor exercise. The general appearance of the insane is fair.

The meals furnished the inmates consist of coffee three times a day, meat twice a day, milk three times a day and

vegetables in abundance. Butter and eggs are also provided.
The beds are clean and supplied with abundant covering.
The inmates generally look after their own rooms.

Bathtubs are provided and all are required to keep clean.
All physically able are free to attend church. The county owns
the farm, and It is well managed. It consists of 237 acres,
with plenty of apples and peaches.

The 1902 report doesn't sound too bad at all. But by 1911, the farm
was condemned because of the poor living conditions. Rats in the walls,
flies everywhere, poor food, and poor ventilation were all to be blamed.

The building that stands today was constructed in 1916. In 1959,
Ashmore Estates Inc. purchased the Poor Farm from Coles County
and began operating as a private psychiatric hospital. By 1965, the hospital made the switch to accepting patients from other state facilities.
In 1979, the Illinois Department of Public Health cited the hospital for
various safety and fire code violations and ordered it to close.

Ashmore Estates was opened in the early 1980s and served as a home
for the mentally disabled. During this period, many patients were known
to be extremely violent, and one woman was even called "possessed" by
one former staff member. The most severe patients were kept on the third
floor. (We found this to be true of every facility we investigated. The idea
is to keep the screams as far away from the administration offices as possible. The superintendent or chief doctor doesn't want to sit in his office
and be bothered by the sounds of the patients.) Financial difficulties led
to the closing of Ashmore in April 1987.

The property was abandoned from 1987 until 2006, when the current owners, Scott and Tanya Kelley, purchased the property for the
purpose of opening a haunted attraction for the Halloween season.

It has been reported that as many as two hundred deaths occurred
on the property. Please refer to Ashmore's website for a link to the grave-
stone photos and list pertaining to the Poor Farm Cemetery. The cemetery is actually on private property, so you won't have access to it when

you go out to investigate. *www.ashmoreestates.net/coles_county_poor_farm _cemetery.htm*

One of the more famous stories that have been televised is that of Elva L. Skinner, a seven-year-old girl who reportedly burned to death in February 1880 when her clothes caught fire in an upstairs room of the former Almshouse. I was able to find the 1880 Mortality Schedule on *www.genealogytrails.com*, and sure enough, little Elva is listed there and it states her cause of death indeed was by fire. I realize the fact that Elva died does not a haunting make. But consider the EVPs that investigators have captured while exploring the top floor of the building, which appear to be a little girl's voice saying, "Mama." Again, not proof of a haunting by Elva. But interesting evidence just the same.

Another famous character is Joe Bloxom, a caretaker of sorts. Many guides and investigators have reported seeing an old man dressed in black wearing a top hat, and the theory is that it is Joe that is still around. His obituary is below:

The *Oakland Messenger Newspaper* (Oakland IL) 2 June 1921 JOE BLOXOM DEAD—Had Been An Inmate of County Almshouse for Many Years

Joe Bloxom, a former resident of Oakland, died at the county poor farm near Ashmore, Wednesday morning and was buried in the cemetery near the farm. Joe had been at the farm a long time and was a willing worker there; taking pride in assisting the superintendent to keep the lawn and grounds clean and tidy. So far as we know, Mr. Bloxom has no living relatives.

In speaking of his death the *Courier* has the following to say:

Joe Bloxom, age 76 years, making the county almshouse his home for fifteen years, died at the home at 10:30 Wednesday morning from injuries believed to have been received between this city and Ashmore some time Tuesday afternoon. Bloxom, who was going to visit in Oakland for a few days, was in Charleston Tuesday and was seen in the railroad districts, near Third street, about noon. It is believed that the man, who was quite feeble, must have been "side swiped" by a train as his shoulders and a part of his body bore severe bruises.

While nothing of a definite nature is known, it is believed that the old man had started to walk to the county farm, after being injured, and was picked up by a passing motorist who left him at the gate of the poor farm about 8:30 on Tuesday night. He was given instant attention by Superintendent Harvey Reigel, who called *physicians,* but the shock and probably the bruises caused the man's death. The *funeral services* were held at the county farm at ten o'clock Thursday morning and burial was made in the "little green plot."

An article in the *Daily Eastern News* (Illinois) in 2007 tells stories from owners Tanya and Scott Kelley about their experiences in Ashmore. The article reported that Scott has heard footsteps when he knew no one was around, and Tanya tells of seeing a photo of a man diving from one of the windows in the front of the building.

Our Experiences—
February 18, 2012, Private Investigation

On February 18, 2012, at around 2:30 p.m., we pulled up to Ashmore Estates and were met by two members of the Mid Illinois Ghost Society, Dustin and Kevin. They were there to let us into the building and give us a brief tour. It was a desolate building in the middle of Illinois farmland, and it was hard to picture any old grandeur. My impression was that it was a sad place.

Kevin told us he was touched by something in the boiler room (possibly Joe Bloxom) and won't go back down there. Some thought-to-be former residents of the poor farm and mental asylum were mentioned to us. Dustin and Kevin pointed out what they thought to be "Mary's Room" on the second floor by the nurse's station as a known hotspot. A small boy (thought to be named Rob or Tim) has been seen from the third-floor window in the room directly behind the nurse's station. People have even pulled off the road to check on the boy! At some point during the tour, I heard a strange noise that startled me. I was told the noise was Pyra, Scott and Tanya's cat. We were told to turn our camera on if we saw Pyra, because reports suggest she will lead you to a spirit. We have always heard that animals are particularly sensitive to picking up on paranormal phenomena.

Having plenty of daylight to explore the location was important to me because I didn't want to get lost when it got dark. While it was daylight, I felt okay wandering off a bit by myself, but still not down to the boiler room (because it was pitch black down there) or even to another floor. I couldn't do it. And when it got dark? I wouldn't let Sam out of my sight.

The "haunt props" from the haunted house were still up, which definitely added to the creepiness of being in this place alone. Decorations for a haunted house, a black maze, and an old piano threw me for a loop on several occasions throughout the night. There was no way I was going to get stuck in any haunted maze! In the afternoon, we could hear a lot of pigeons on the roof cooing (the roof is in the process of being restored), so this obstructed us somewhat, but they were silent when it got dark. There are also many open windows, and believe me, the wind was whipping through the place. It was probably twenty-eight degrees that day.

We had some interesting experiences on the third floor. The first thing that springs to mind is that despite our numerous attempts, we could not open the door to the third-floor room (the one connected to the story of the boy) that Dustin and Kevin showed us on our tour. Our camera's batteries were repeatedly drained, which is a common complaint associated with paranormal activity. The spirits are thought to draw energy this way. Thankfully, we had plenty of backup batteries because we seemed to use all of them, and the K2 was lighting up like crazy throughout the evening—all the way to red. We heard several loud bangs, but we attributed them to the wind.

On the second floor, where the piano prop is located, we also had seemingly responsive K2 activity—the device would light up to different colors when Sam would ask it to. However, I never felt anything while experiencing the K2 activity. As in, I never sensed a presence or got goosebumps.

The best piece of evidence we obtained from Ashmore Estates was a piece of video taken in the boiler room of our flashlights turning on and off. Before Sam turned the camera on, the K2 was lighting up all the way to red. Reviewing our voice recorder, I said to Sam, "The dark is playing tricks on my eyes. You know why? Because I'm looking at that light, and it seems to get dimmer. Or just the area in front of me or something? Blacker than black, I guess is how to describe it." Then I said out loud to whatever or whoever I thought I was seeing, "Am I looking at you? Am I seeing you?" And then back to Sam: "It's too dark, I don't like it." Within thirty seconds, Sam and I were gasping because the flashlight turned on, and Sam claimed that the flashlight was rolling back and forth.

An excerpt from the transcript of the video session is below:

- ME: We'll wait for you. (Twenty-second pause) Concentrate with me. I'm going to count to ten and I want you to really give everything that you've got, to turn that flashlight on when we get to ten. Turn it on. I can tell that you're here. Thank you for trying to talk to us.
  - » Lights up.

- ME: Thank you so much. Can you turn it right back off for me? Just twist it right back off. All right, I'm going to ask you a question, and it's only going to work if we use turning the flashlight on for a yes, so you have to turn it back off before we can play.
  - » Light turns off.

• SAM: It may be hard for whoever we're talking to, to turn it on and off. May not be able to do it.

• ME: It seems to be very hard.

• SAM: Because it's taking a long time for, I mean, if we've been dealing with the same person the whole time we've been here. We're not disappointed or anything. You can turn it on anytime you want to. If it's hard, if it takes a lot of energy, that's fine.

• ME: The thing that we find, and it may be because it's on that surface, I don't know if that has anything to do with it, I don't know why it would, but in our experience, we've seen that blue flashlight go off very quickly in response to our questions.
» Lights up.

• ME: We weren't trying to insult you. That's incredible. Can you turn on any of the other ones? The purple or the black one?

• SAM: There are two more over there.

• ME: See what you can do with those two other ones. I don't care which one. I just want to see. I feel like I can tell that you're trying to do it. That's so good. If you can't get those to work, that's fine. You can keep using the blue one, and we'll know that you tried and those are just too hard to work.
» Lights up.

• ME: Is it okay that we're here?
» Lights up.

• ME: Are you still here with us?

» Lights up.

Of course, I'm kicking myself now for not directly asking, "Is this Elva, Mary, Tim, Rob, or Joe?" But we did ask all of those questions utilizing the K2 meter and did not get any hits. The takeaway from this session to me is this—if you think you see something, maybe you really did see something. So try to back up what you think you saw by capturing it on a voice recorder or on video like we did down in the boiler room here.

We don't know who or what is haunting Ashmore Estates, but we definitely had some interesting personal experiences. I look forward to visiting it again in the summer or fall. Or whenever it isn't twenty-eight degrees outside!

The boiler room where we captured the video of the flashlight turning on and off, seemingly in response to our questions.

If You Decide to Visit:

Location & Contact Info

22645 E. CR 1050N

Ashmore, IL 61912

Tel: 217-495-2495 or 217-459-1359

Email: *info@ashmoreestates.net*

Owners: Scott and Tanya Kelley

Website

www.ashmoreestates.net

Type of Tours/Hunts Offered

Flashlight tours and overnight private investigations.

Haunted attraction for Halloween? Yes

Bathroom facilities? No

Safe room for sleeping/snacking? No

Size: 15,000 sq. ft., three floors, two staircases to utilize.

Price: $60 per person for a four-hour investigation ($300 minimum); overnights are $80 per person ($600 minimum).

Tips: Get to know KFC and Walmart because that is where you will be making your bathroom runs.

Closest airports: Indianapolis International Airport—101 miles away; St. Louis International Airpot—130 miles away; Louisville International Airport—150 miles away; and Chicago airports are about 160 miles away.

Media Appearances

Ghost Adventures, Season 5, Episode 1—9/23/11

Ghost Hunters, Season 9, Episode 4—2/6/13

Syfy's *Children of the Grave II*, DVD Release Date—4/15/12

Sam's Observations

Ashmore was an interesting experience. For whatever reason, we've discovered that boiler rooms are the go-to spots for paranormal activity. We've caught EVPs and had flashlight responses, as well as shadow play in most of the boiler rooms we have visited.

Maybe it was the cold, but I was thinking that this night was going to be a bust. As we were sitting in the frigid, dark boiler room, Jamie started noticing part of the room getting darker. As soon as she voiced this observation to me, one of our flashlights turned on! I felt a sense of disbelief, excitement, relief, and validation, all at once.

This journey that we were embarking on together was getting off to a great start!

TWO

WAVERLY HILLS—
LOUISVILLE, KENTUCKY

The original structure that was used for the tuberculosis hospital was built in 1910. The building that stands now was completed in 1926 and was designed to care for four hundred patients. Waverly remained open until 1961. The last remaining patients were transferred on June 1 of that year to Hazelwood Sanatorium. No, it wasn't closed due to patient abuse. Waverly Hills was closed because a cure was finally developed!

Woodhaven Geriatrics Center operated in this building from 1962 until 1980, when it was finally closed down by the state amid rumors of patient neglect and mistreatment. The building remained empty until 2001, when Charles and Tina Mattingly purchased it.

By all accounts, Waverly was a modern facility that attracted people from all over the world. The hospital finally had to limit patients to residents of Jefferson County. A 1955 article from the *Courier-Journal* (Louisville, KY) described Waverly as a cheerful place. People came here with a common goal—either to be cured or to provide help to cure others.

Here is an excerpt from the *Courier-Journal* that painted a loving picture of Waverly and its strong connection and impact to the community from the time it opened until the middle of the twentieth century:

Datestamp: 11/23/1989

A PLACE IN TIME; WAVERLY HILLS; TUBERCULOSIS HOSPITAL WAS HEART OF AN ISOLATED COMMUNITY, INSPIRING LOYALTY IN PATIENTS.

When the hospital opened in 1911, it had 8 patients, but it soon reached its capacity of 40. At the time, Jefferson County had one of the country's highest rates of tuberculosis, a highly contagious, sometimes fatal lung disease characterized by coughing, hemorrhaging, fever, and shortness of breath.

And the hospital, which offered plenty of bed rest and fresh air as well as some surgical methods of treating the disease, was thought to be an excellent facility. In 1924, the hospital was expanded to house 400 patients.

Many people died at the hospital, and because hospital officials were concerned that the sight of hearses would be bad for morale, the bodies were sent to the bottom of the hill through a steam tunnel.

The steam kept the tunnel warm and was also used by employees who needed to walk up the hill during the winter. [Longtime area resident Kenneth Wade] Fey remembers that he and other children would go into the tunnel to warm up after sledding.

In addition to the fond recollections as a "quiet, woodsy backdrop for the neighborhood," the article chronicled Waverly Hill's ups and downs. This included the hospital closing in 1961, as the development of streptomycin allowed more patients to be treated at home. The remaining patients were transferred to Hazelwood Tuberculosis Sanatorium in the South End. Another dark era ended when the state closed down the nursing home at Waverly Hills in 1980, allegedly for poor patient care.

The article also noted the bleak conditions of Waverly's buildings, which included rampant vandalism as they awaited plans for redevelopment.

> But the current silence and emptiness of the Waverly Hills grounds belies the memories that employees have of that place.
>
> Douglas Steele remembers it fondly as a place that changed his life.
>
> He entered thinking he didn't have much chance to live. He was a patient for more than five years, but when he left the hospital he was healthy and married, and he had a new career. He worked in the radiology department after he recovered and works with the county health department today.
>
> And when the Steeles remember the hospital, they talk of people playing practical jokes on each other and patients reportedly sneaking out to go to concerts. They remember a community filled with life and laughter and visitors.

Yes, there were exploratory/experimental surgeries done here on the fourth floor. These were paid operations that people wanted because it was their best chance to live. Thoracoplasty and artificial pneumothorax were two of the procedures used. The National Institutes of Health explains thoracoplasty as a procedure whereby several ribs are removed in order to make the lungs collapse, which causes disfigurement. The idea was that if you removed the ribs over the diseased portion of the lungs, you could help preserve the functioning of the nondiseased areas. Artificial pneumothorax is when the lung is manually collapsed using air.

Outside of these operations, the treatments were basically just sun, food, air, and rest. That was all they had to fight the disease. It wasn't until Streptomycin was developed in 1944 that doctors actually had an antibiotic to fight tuberculosis.

March 3, 2012 Historical Guided Tour
7:00–9:00 p.m. and
Public Full Night Investigation/Ghost Hunt
12:00–8:00 a.m.

I would recommend the historical tour to anyone in the area—even to those with no interest in the paranormal. The full night investigation/ghost hunt might not be as appealing to all. However, I found this place so interesting that I intend to make another visit to Waverly for one of the daytime tours, which are conducted one Sunday each month.

We had to leave the property after the historical tour was over, but we arrived back on site about 11:45 p.m. for our ghost hunt. We lined up behind a row of other cars waiting to get in the gates. The waiting and the security measures combined to produce a very eerie sense of anticipation. When we made it to the top of the hill, there was a man checking people in when we drove up to the gate. Everyone got their equipment out of their cars and was taking photos of the building. The sheer size and reputation of Waverly is awe-inspiring. Once everyone was sort of standing around in the same spot in the parking area, we were led down by a guide to (what was once used as) the laundry room to sign our waivers and begin the orientation. There is a small gift shop and museum set up in the laundry room. There were plenty of long tables and chairs for teams to claim for an area to store the items they weren't going to carry in with them. We were split into groups of ten, and guides rotated us throughout the floors. We really liked the way the public hunt was conducted. The check-in process was efficient, and we got started very close to on time (which is very hard to do with a group of people). The guides gave us a brief rundown of stories/history before letting us loose anywhere, and the transitions between floors went smoothly. If you had to go to the bathroom, someone would walk you down and return you to your floor so you wouldn't get lost. They cap the public events to fifty people, and it really is almost like having a private hunt. The only time you feel that you are attending a public event is when you get to the fifth floor—and that is only because this is the partial floor, so you're all confined to a much smaller area.

Our Experiences

The Body Chute

On the historical tour, the group we were assigned to visited the Body Chute, a.k.a. the "Death Tunnel," first. We were guilty of a preconceived notion that I'm sure a lot of visitors have. We thought this was built for the sole purpose of moving the deceased out of the hospital. Not so. This tunnel was built for bringing supplies up the hill, and employees also utilized it to walk up the hill to work and stay out of the cold. It was only when the death toll started getting so high that the tunnel was used for moving bodies.

It is said that only one hearse ever pulled up to the front of the building. The hospital administrators are attributed to saying that they thought the hearses pulling up would adversely affect the patients' morale. They didn't want the patients to see how many deaths were occurring.

We were allowed to walk on the steps all the way to the bottom of the tunnel. Until you are walking back up, you don't realize how far down you are. So be forewarned. It is a hike back up to the top of that tunnel! But it's an experience like no other. It is absolutely haunting, and it will make you pause and think about the people who climbed those stairs to get to work every day while bodies were being moved down the conveyor belt on their left to be picked up by a hearse at the bottom of the hill or to be loaded on a train and taken back to their families for burial. Victims of the "White Plague."

First Floor

This is where the morgue is. We were told that the tables are period specific, but on loan and not original to Waverly.

Second Floor

People have reported phantom smells. Bread baking, pancakes, etc.

Third Floor

There have been several stories associated with this floor that have appeared
on popular ghost investigation shows on television. Rumors abound about
Timmy and Mary, two of the resident ghost children who have been known
to move toy balls around. Allegedly, in the 1980s, a homeless man and his
dog were found murdered in an elevator. The story is that it was some type
of gang-related killing and that the eyes were cut out of both the man and
the dog. The elevator rests on the third floor. The man has reportedly been
seen (appearing with no eyes), and people have reported that they have
chased a phantom dog around the building—only to have it disappear.

Fourth Floor

This is where it gets a little unsettling, to say the least. Make sure you
hear about the teenage boys, their axe, and the fascinating shadow people
who terrorized them and would not let them leave. Hands down, this is
the most notorious floor at Waverly. There are countless stories of people
experiencing the shadow people phenomenon.

HUNTING SHADOW PEOPLE ON THE HISTORICAL TOUR

While on the historical tour, our group gathered close together while our
guide directed us to focus our eyes on the ground. He told us to watch the
light coming in the windows and to sort of watch for something to break
the light, but not to look directly at it.

Next, he asked for volunteers to walk down the long, dark hallway
alone. Sam was the first one to go. He was told to turn back, face the group,
and to walk back slowly. Several members of the group said they saw Sam's

shadow on the left and some other mystery shadow that was following him on his right side! One man yelled out, "Jesus Christ, I just saw it!"

Several of the guys took this opportunity to walk down the dark hallway, taking turns one at a time, until finally our guide realized that no females had done it yet, so he started teasing us a little bit. I volunteered (or maybe Sam volunteered me, actually, now that I think back on it) to walk down the hallway beside another girl. Yes, my heart was about to beat out of my chest—even though I knew I was safe. Even though I knew there was no reason at all for me to be experiencing any fear, I still felt it. There were about fifteen other people within a few feet of me. But still, I was so scared that I almost couldn't do it. That hallway is no joke.

When the two of us turned to walk back, people were gasping. I am told that the two of us were seen walking with two shadows on either side of us and one in the middle of us. I didn't feel anything or sense anything while this was going on, but I will tell you that I didn't turn my head to look in either direction. I froze my head and line of vision to focus on walking back to Sam and didn't look back or to the side, or anywhere else for that matter. I was very much acting like a horse with blinders on.

Once we made it to the stairwell and were preparing to go up to the fifth floor, I asked Sam, "Did you see anything with me?" He replied, "Yes, something was on both sides of you, and something was in between you. Yep. Surely did. But it didn't creep me out as bad as when I saw something just run—right behind that girl." Suffice it to say—I'm pretty much still glad that I didn't look around, although I would be willing to go up there by myself in the light of day. Probably. Maybe. As long as someone was waiting for me on the stairwell entrance to this floor!

Hunting Shadow People on Our Own

Later that evening, we had the opportunity to explore the fourth floor on our own during the ghost hunt. I can remember our guide standing with us in the stairwell outside the door to the fourth floor. He was telling us some of the history and stories from other ghost hunters, staff, and security guards over the years. When our guide finished talking, he posed the question to our group: "So, who wants to be the first ones on this floor?" There was dead silence for several seconds as we all looked at each other, looked at the ground, and looked at the ceiling. Then Sam opened his mouth and volunteered us. "We'll go," he said. I almost kicked him. He must have sensed that, because he hurried away from me into the depths of the hallway. And I had no choice but to keep up or be left behind. Needless to say, I kept up as we plunged forward into the darkness.

I sat in the hallway (with my back to the wall, because obviously this keeps me safe from ghosts), and Sam stood like a crazy person would, exposing his back to the open hallway behind us. We settled in and we just watched our surroundings for about thirty minutes. I didn't see anything, and we didn't have any flashlight activity going on, but Sam said he saw a shadow dart back and forth from one room into the other at the end of the hallway. Being in that hallway in the dark was very creepy. There was a heaviness in the air that you almost feel like you can cut through with your bare hands. It was difficult at times for me to breathe. (Note: Looking back, I think this feeling may demonstrate my characteristics as an empath. I didn't think anything of it at the time. But geez…I had problems breathing in a TB hospital?! Interesting. Sam did not have this same experience.) Sitting out in the solarium and thinking about the rows and rows of patient beds that used to line that area is also a chilling experience.

Sam believes we captured the following EVP in the fourth-floor hallway:

  • ME: Is there anybody that wants to talk to us? We sure would like to see you or hear from you. We've come a long way from Atlanta, Georgia.

  » RESPONSE: **Hi**…(twenty-one seconds later) **Hey**…

WHAT ARE SHADOW PEOPLE?

What causes this shadow phenomenon? We were on the fourth floor of the building—there are no trees up there that high and nothing else that we could see that would cast a shadow. And what kind of trees cast shadows that appear to dart in and out of doorways? What kind of shadows run? What are shadow people? We don't know. There are theories that range from positing that the shadow people are interdimensional time travelers from a parallel universe or that they are demons, ghosts, or possibly an effect created by our subconscious minds. In *Ghosts and Spirits*, by Rosemary Ellen Guiley, under her entry for shadow people, she writes that "they find ways into the physical world and seem to have the purpose-unknown-of observing humans. They may show up as bedroom visitors because the nature of human sleeping or dreaming consciousness enables an entry for them. Their appearance may be a form they deliberately assume, or it may be the only way they can manifest in the physical realm." Whatever they are, they are fascinating to watch for.

We were also told that if you shine your light at the shadows, your light won't penetrate them. So whatever they are, they allegedly have mass. Seeing something out of the corner of your eye is one thing. It is very easy to dismiss that as an optical illusion. But what about when you see it right in front of you? Go to Waverly and conduct your own experiments. I would love to hear your theories on what this is.

Fifth Floor

On the historical tour, we heard that at one time there was a swing set up here on the roof for the children. We were also told that if TB spread to your brain, it could drive you insane, and those patients were kept up here. We were told that years ago, a security guard stayed alone up here one night in a tent. He was surrounded by the sound of footsteps walking around his tent and even had something poking at the tent. He was found sitting, holding the tent when the sun came up, and then vowed to never go up to the fifth floor again!

This is also the location of possibly the most infamous room in the building—room 502. Many rumors and stories have circulated about what happened to a pregnant nurse up here. One version claims that she was depressed from all the sickness and death, and she hanged herself. Another version claims she was pregnant by a married doctor, performed an abortion on herself, and then hanged herself. Perhaps the most chilling version is that the doctor performed the abortion on her, it went wrong and she died, and the hanging was staged as a cover-up. Take the historical tour, read Patti Starr's section on Waverly in *Ghosthunting Kentucky*, and pay attention to what John Thornberry has to say in the Booth Brothers Documentary entitled *Spooked*. It makes sense to me that it would be something that people would want kept secret and that no documents exist because of that desire to bury the event. There is another popular media rumor about a nurse leaping out a window to her death from this room.

We did get an interesting photo of what appears to be a lightning bolt sort of shape outside room 502 while we were on the public tour. We got several interesting photos of lightning bolt shapes throughout the building. I don't know if it is paranormal, but I can tell you that in all my years of snapping photographs, I have never experienced this effect before, since, or anywhere else. Make of that what you will.

We conducted an EVP session in the famous room 502, and about three minutes in to our session, I say, "I'm not feeling it. I think all the visitors have chased out all the spirits. They're not amused by us tonight." And then you hear a raspy voice of a man, as if he is struggling to get out all of the words, say: **"I don't see it happening."** Everyone else in our group was on the other side of the fifth floor out on the roof. We believe it to be a Class A EVP that we caught there that night. It amazes us! We also captured a second EVP while in room 502:

- ME: Anybody want to say, "I'm here?" I'm here!
  » RESPONSE: **Yeah.**

We were freezing cold all night, not Waverly's fault of course. One of our theories about ghost hunting is that it may be harder to capture evidence in the cold. Why? Because energy moves faster through denser air? It is important to me to point out that of everywhere we visited, Waverly was the only place where we were unable to get anything whatsoever to happen with our flashlights. We also think it has to do with our ability to concentrate and keep our minds focused and open. This is hard to do if all you can think about is staying warm. Another visit to Waverly, next time during the summer months, is going to be a must.

We also figured that it is harder to capture evidence on a public hunt. Well, a visit to St. Albans just a few weeks later proved us wrong about that theory!

If You Decide to Visit:

Location & Contact Info

4400 Paralee Lane
Louisville, KY 40272
Tel: 502-933-2142
Email: *info@therealwaverlyhills.com*
Owners: Charles and Tina Mattingly

Website

www.therealwaverlyhills.com

Type of Tours/Hunts Offered

Private and public ghost hunts, daytime and nighttime two-hour historical tours

Haunted attraction for Halloween? Yes

Bathroom facilities? Yes—and they get our award for best bathrooms!

Safe room for sleeping/snacking? Yes, but more of a hangout room.

Size: 180,000 sq. ft., four floors, with a partial fifth floor.

Price: $100 per person for full-night public hunt; call for pricing on private hunts.

Tips: Stay at the Brown Hotel and order a Hot Brown!

Closest airports: Louisville International Airport.

Media Appearances

ABC Family's *Scariest Places on Earth*—7/19/01

Death Tunnel, Sony Pictures—2/28/06

Ghost Hunters, Season 2, Episode 24—3/29/06

Spooked—6/7/06

VH1's *Celebrity Paranormal Project*

Ghost Hunters, Season 3, Episode 318—11/7/07

Ghost Hunters Academy—6/2/10

Ghost Adventures, Season 4, Episode 30—10/8/10

Paranormal Challenge—7/22/11

Ghost Hunters, Season 7, Episode 722—11/9/11

Sam's Observations

Waverly Hills was on my "bucket list" of haunted places to visit. The stories of Waverly have been well documented on television. I can recite them almost verbatim. We drove up to it at dusk, and the building is awe inspiring. For a ghost enthusiast, I assume it's a similar feeling mountain climbers experience when they first see the base of Mt. Everest. Exhilaration.

While on the historical tour, we were led into the "Shadow Hallway." Our guide asked for a volunteer, and I jumped at the chance. My hand is always raised first because I want to experience all that I can. I was told to walk about fifty feet down the hallway away from our group. My instructions were to stop, turn around, and walk slowly back. I didn't experience anything for myself, but others in our group saw shadows moving around and behind me.

Jamie and another female in our group were asked to do the same thing together (neither wanted to do it by themselves). When they walked back, they didn't walk back alone! There were five shadow people with them. Two were on either side, and one was between the two ladies.

It's hard to say if this was an optical illusion or something paranormal. It was an interesting sight nonetheless. I have never seen anything like it before or since.

THREE

St. Albans Sanatorium — Radford, Virginia

This parcel of land itself is no stranger to bloodshed, being the site of several Civil War battles. The buildings first housed a school for boys, which opened on September 19, 1892, and closed in 1911. The buildings remained empty until Dr. J. C. King purchased them in 1915 and founded St. Albans Sanatorium, a private psychiatric hospital that received its first patients on January 16, 1916. On page 28 of Monty S. Leitch's *In Appreciation of a Distinct Need*, Dr. James P. King is quoted from a 1962 speech describing his father's vision for the hospital:

Psychiatry, at the turn of the century, consisted primarily of what we would term custodial care. The vast majority of patients were treated in state hospitals during an era when one hospital vied with another for the lowest cost per patient per day. Dr. John C. King...had the idea that better care for the mentally ill would result in a higher percentage of recoveries. He was a man of the older school of medicine, dedicated to his work and willing to risk his professional career on the assumption that a private hospital would find acceptance in this area.

In St. Albans' earliest days, the treatments fixated on good food (fresh from their own farm and said to be served by a waiter on a table set with fresh linens and silver flatware), rest, massage, electricity, outdoor activities, and hydrotherapy.

An anonymous and frightening 1927 committed patient record reads: "Has seen angels; has heard strange voices, and voices of dead."

You mean people got sent away for that?! Good grief, Sam and I would be sent up the river immediately!

Beginning in the mid-1940s, St. Albans began utilizing sub-coma insulin shock and electroconvulsive therapies (ECT). On page 44, Ms. Leitch describes such therapies:

In sub-coma insulin shock treatments, the patient was given increasingly large doses of insulin to reduce the sugar content of the blood and bring on coma. After about an hour, the coma was terminated, either with an infusion of saline solution by stomach tube or with an intravenous injection of glucose. In ECT, alternating electric current was passed through the brain by electrodes attached at the patient's temples. This produced unconsciousness and seizure, which had the effect of relieving severe depression or psychosis and enabling psychotherapy.

St. Albans Sanatorium.

These treatments were effecting to a degree, but often resulted in physical and mental complications, inluding some deaths. The insulin therapy stopped in 1967, but ECT therapy is still utilized, albeit in a modified version that is deemed safer.

It was claimed that in the hospital's later years, it received the most difficult patients that other state hospitals couldn't handle. Unfortunately, St. Albans has had its share of suicides as well.

St. Albans became a part of the Carilion Health System in the 1990s and was eventually closed in 2004, when Carilion gave it to Radford University.

March 31, 2012—Public Ghost Hunt

Prior to the hunt, we were allowed to walk around the lobby and first floor and take photos. The size of the building will deceive you. I was captivated by the restoration of the gorgeous staircase and the hardwood floors in the main building. You can still tell without using much imagination just how beautiful the campus must have been in its glory days. We were able to speak with several members of the Mountain Ridge Paranormal Research Society (MRPRS), a local paranormal group whose members have worked to save St. Albans and preserve its history.

We met Jessica Wright, administrator and member of MRPRS, prior to the event. Her father, Barry, who is also a member of MRPRS, spoke with us at length about some of the history and paranormal reports that he has personally experienced and heard from other groups coming in over the years.

Some reported experiences include full-body apparitions, most notably a woman walking through the hall carrying a baby, and a girl with long black hair. Shadow people have been seen throughout the building—both walking and crawling ("creepers")—and something that has red eyes has also been sighted. There is also something that is believed to be nonhuman. An evil entity. And no, it is not confined to the boiler room. It goes where it wants. Several people have been scratched and burned. One man had welts show up on his back. They disappeared within an hour, but he said he felt as though his back was on fire!

A beautiful staircase that has been restored. Just under the archway, a full-body apparition of a woman carrying a baby has been spotted.

I knew that MRPRS is a faith-based organization and very much wanted to hear their perspective on the paranormal happenings at St. Albans. I felt comfortable asking Barry what he thought caused all this seemingly paranormal type activity? He brought up a Bible verse in Luke, which I found when I got home, among others:

Luke 24:39: Look at my hands and my feet. It is I myself! Touch me and see; a ghost does not have flesh and bones, as you see I have.

Matthew 14:26: But when the disciples saw him walking on the sea, they were terrified, and said, "It is a ghost!" and they cried out in fear.

1 Thessalonians 4:13—18: But I do not want you to be ignorant, brethren, concerning those who have fallen asleep, lest you sorrow as others who have no hope. For if we believe that Jesus died and rose again, even so God will bring with Him those who sleep in Jesus.

For this we say to you by the word of the Lord, that we who are alive and remain until the coming of the Lord will by no means precede those who are asleep. For the Lord Himself will descend from heaven with a shout, with the voice of an archangel, and with the trumpet of God. And the dead in Christ will rise first. Then we who are alive and remain shall be caught up together with them in the clouds to meet the Lord in the air. And thus we shall always be with the Lord. Therefore comfort one another with these words.

Wow! These verses intrigued me because they really give credence to the idea that our spirits maybe don't immediately go to heaven or hell. That we are "asleep" and our spirits are here—traveling around just like we do in life, until the coming of the Lord. Barry said that they've had reports that support that theory—Christian relatives who have passed on and shown up and made themselves known at St. Albans. That the place is a beacon of sorts. He said, "Think about it. If you were a spirit who had something to say, where would you go?" I replied, "To a place where people are trying to hear me." Exactly!

Another thing we spoke about is how to shield yourself. Barry told us that nothing beats the power of prayer. He also said, "Don't open yourself up to anything. Don't ask something to touch you."

We really appreciated the conversation we had with Barry. He gave us a lot of new ideas to think about.

Our Experiences

After Jessica gave the group an orientation, we were released to explore on our own. There were no assigned groups and no rotations for hotspot areas. We were all given free rein. We did not get a tour of the building first. Members of MRPRS were stationed throughout the building to provide assistance if you had questions or got lost. At first I thought this was a little strange, but once we got going, I actually loved this format.

The building (to me, anyway) was intuitively designed, and I did not get turned around. Things were where I thought they should be. Being able to roam freely helped build the excitement and sense of adventure. The first place we went to was the boiler room.

Boiler Room

Sam set the flashlights down on the floor and stepped away. The blue one turned on but wouldn't turn back off. Nothing was responding to our questions. I stomped around the flashlights to see if I could get anything to turn on or off, but nothing happened. At one point, Sam panned the camera over to me because I said, "I swear, something just breathed in my ear." We began seeing a purplish light in the upper corner of the room. There was no way that it could have been a camera flash! We took turns going into the room next door and shining our flashlights up to the ceiling to see if we could replicate this effect. We could not. Later, when we got home, we saw a photo on the MRPRS website of a purple-light phenomenon upstairs that was exactly what we saw in the boiler room! We also learned that a maintenance man was electrocuted down here, and an electrician had a heart attack and died down here.

Boiler room where we were seeing a mysterious purplish light in the top left corner of this photo. I went in the room next door and shined a light up at the top of the wall, but we were unable to replicate what we were seeing. We don't know what it was. Also, this is the room where I thought I was talking to a suicide victim.

Purple Room

We heard our first audible disembodied voice up here. We walked in the room and Sam said, "Smells old." I said, "Smells insane." We then heard some man with a deep voice laughing at us. We heard it right out loud when it happened, too, not later when we got home and listened to our voice recorder. There was no one outside the window—no one anywhere around us that could have made that noise. For the critics out there, I will admit that there is a possibility that maybe someone downstairs was the source of the laughter, and it somehow traveled up to us through an air vent. I guess. It sure did serve to creep us out, though, whatever it was.

Attic

This was a fun place to explore, although nothing much happened to us up here. Once again, we lined our flashlights up in a row, and this time, the purple one turned itself on after we stepped away. I said, "I think something is just following us around turning this light on. Trying to mess with us."

Suicide Room

We had heard a story through one of the paranormal television shows about a woman who had a miscarriage but was allowed to keep her baby in a jar in the closet. There are chairs in this room, and Sam and I were glad to sit down. Just a few minutes into our session, I started getting chills all over my body. I said, "I've never sat in a place and just had chills. I'm not scared, it's not cold in here. (Note: On our voice recorder, you can hear a male voice repeating after me, "Cold in here.") I feel like something's going on." This was just after Sam asked if anyone was here with us. Within seconds, I was overcome with the desire to cry—and not just sit in the chair and have tears stream down my face. The desire was to go in the corner and curl into a ball and weep openly. I got out of there pretty quickly after I started feeling that way. It was a very strange experience, and I believe I was somehow feeling a woman's heart break.

Dragon Room (Home of the Ghost Who Told Us to Leave/ I Ain't Too Proud to Beg Flashlight Session)

We captured our first responsive flashlight session of the evening in this room. You can tell in the video how excited I was, and I guess maybe I was being a little obnoxious and cocky about it, sort of bouncing around and prancing a little. At this point, this type of experience was still fairly new to us, so capturing it on video just blew our minds. Sam and I were down here trying to do the flashlight experiment. I had all three lights lined up next to each other in a row. After a few minutes, I decided to move the purple light farther away from us, closer to the wall with the dragon artwork. Almost immediately, the light turned on. The transcript of this session is as follows:

· ME: We've got to play the game some more. You've got to turn it back on. Can you please turn it back on for us? I know, I know. You're not my monkey. But will you play for just a second? Thank you for trying to talk to us. That's pretty cool what you're doing. But the thing about doing it once is that you've got to do it twice. I think you just want to hear me beg. Please, please, please, turn that flashlight on. Maybe you want to hear Sam beg. Beg, Sam.

· SAM: Can you, uh, please turn that on for us?

· ME: Sam's not really saying it like he means it.

· SAM: I am, I just don't want to bother anybody else.

· ME: You've got my complete attention.

· SAM: We'll stick around for a bit if you want us to.

· ME: Where'd you go? We're listening. We're waiting on you. Are you still with us? Turn that light back on if you're still with us. Are we talking to a male? Can you turn that light on?
» Lights up.

· ME: Wow. Okay, turn it back off for me. I'm going to ask you some more questions if you feel like playing. If the answer's yes, then you'll turn the light back on. Does that sound good? You want to play? You want to talk to us?

· SAM: You've got to turn the light off all the way in order to answer a question, okay? Thank you.

· ME: All right, so you said you're male. The next thing that we want to know is are you a child? Turn that light back on.
» Light turns off.

• ME: Okay, if you're not a child, that means that you're an adult, right? What are you trying to tell me here? (Mumbling to Sam): What does it mean if it doesn't turn the light back on?

• SAM (mumbling back): I don't know, Jamie. I don't know how hard it is to manipulate.

• ME: Um … Is turning the light on really hard for you? Does it take a lot of energy?

• ME: How about this one … Are you always here?

• ME: If you're not always here …
  » Lights up.

• ME: Can you tell us in the recorder where you go when you're not here?

• SAM: Why do you come here?

• ME: Were you a patient here?

• SAM (mumbling to me): They said they were just passing through.

• ME: Are you from Virginia?

• ME: Are you from a different state other than Virginia?
  » Lights up.

• ME: So you're from another state. Well tell us in the recorder what you're doing in Virginia. We came up here pretty much just to talk to you.

• SAM: Yeah, we came all the way from Atlanta, Georgia.

• ME: Well do you like it here? I'm having a good time myself. Do you know anybody here?
» Lights up.

• ME: Can you turn it back off? Thank you. Man, I sure do like talking to you. I'm serious. You're making my night. You really are. Okay, so do you know any of the paranormal teams here? Is that who you know?

• ME: Do you know other spirits here?

• ME: Okay. You're gonna laugh at me when I ask you this, but I'm really serious. I really want to know this question. Do you miss eating? Like, do you miss getting to get something good to eat? You don't miss it? That gives me a little peace. I really worry that I'm going to miss out on the eating.
» Lights up.

• ME: Uh-oh. Is that a—I feel your pain, Jamie. I used to like to get something good to eat, too? What does that mean? Can you turn it back off and I'm going to ask you to confirm again about the missing eating. Because it really troubles me. See, when I was a little kid, one of the things that they would tell us in church was when you pass and go to heaven, you won't miss any of the earthly stuff. You won't miss sleep, you won't … you know, miss food, you won't miss any of that stuff. But I don't know. I really like to eat. And I really like to get a good night's sleep. So tell me, really, do you miss getting something good to eat? Okay. Hopefully I won't miss it either. It worries me.

• ME: What about the sleep thing? Do you sleep now? I don't know.

• ME: Do you get irritated with some of these ghost hunters that come in? Do you get tired of answering questions? I work for lawyers and I get tired of answering their questions. All they do is yap at me and ask me stuff.

» Lights up.

• ME: I know, it's irritating. Sometimes you just don't feel like answering questions anymore. Well, can you turn it back off?

• SAM: Can you please turn it off for me?

• BOTH: Thank you.

• ME: Well I think it's okay that we're here because you keep talking to us. It's cool that we're here, right? Okay, you're hurting my feelings. I said—it's okay that we're here, right? C'mon man. I feel like I'm fifteen years old waiting for my date to pick me up. Did you just dump me? Are we done here?

• SAM: Can you turn it on one more time—if you want us to leave?

• ME: Is it time for us to go?

» Lights up.

• SAM: Okay.

• ME: All right. Thank you. We're headed out.

- SAM: Thank you for talking with us, we appreciate it. If you'll turn it off again we'll come pick it up and we'll leave you alone.

- ME: Thank you for your time. We really appreciate it.

What I took from this session was that we were speaking with some-one who told us that he wasn't always there (though I neglected to clar-ify what "there" meant), that he knew someone at St. Albans, and that he gets irritated with answering ghost hunters' questions! Then he very clearly indicated to us that it was time for us to go. What I wonder about now, though, is if he was telling us to go to protect us from something else coming through to us, or if he was tired of us and wanted to be left alone. But regardless, if something I can't see tells me it's time to go, I'm inclined to heed that advice! As my dad would say, it was "time to beat feet." We hoofed it out of there.

After this session, we returned upstairs and were able to listen in on a session that Chuck (a member of MRPRS) was doing in the Suicide Room and were able to see a session that he did using dowsing rods. It was sometime during the dowsing rod session in the hallway just at the bottom of the attic stairs that Sam witnessed his first (and to date—only) apparition.

The Ghost Face Thriller Hallway. This is where Sam
saw a white face with black eyes peek out at him.

Return to the Boiler Room

Our last stop for the night was to return to the boiler room. We were warned to be careful—there was a report of a girl getting scratched that night! We returned and got settled in. Same as before—we laid the lights out on the ground and one came on immediately. Here is the transcript for what followed:

- ME: Just to be sure that's you and I don't have a crazy flashlight, can you turn that light back off for me?
  » Light turns off.

- ME: Wow, that's incredible. Okay, so we'll ask you a question and if the answer is yes, then you'll turn the light back on. Does that work for you? Can we do it that way? Do you want to try to talk to us?
  » Lights up.

- SAM: Can you try to turn another flashlight on? There are two others there.

- ME: Are we talking to a male?

- ME: That must mean we're talking to a female.

- ME: Are we talking to something else?
  » Lights up.

- ME (mumbling): I don't know if I like this anymore.

- SAM: Can you try to turn on another flashlight, please? We'll leave you alone if you'll turn on another flashlight.

• ME: Don't say that! I want to talk. Sam will leave you alone. Ain't that just like a man. I would like to talk to you. Just as long as you would like to talk to me. Ain't that just like a man?

» Lights up.

• ME: Yeah! Thank you. Okay, I have a different question if you'll turn it back off.

» Light turns off.

• ME: Were you down here with us earlier tonight? Different question. Do you like it here? (We have an EVP that says "**yes**" immediately after this question.) Are you stuck here?

» Lights up.

• ME: Can you tell us, in the recorder, why? Turn that light back off for me and I'm going to ask a follow-up question, okay?

» Light turns off.

• ME: If you're stuck here, do you know why?

• ME: Okay, that means you don't know why? Is that right? You don't know?

» Lights up.

• ME: Okay, make it go dark again.

» Light turns off.

• SAM: Can you please try to turn on another flashlight when you get that one turned off?

• SAM: Do you know how long you've been stuck here?

• SAM: Does it feel like a long time?

» Lights up.

- ME: Okay, turn it back off. I hear some other people coming. Don't go away. Don't leave us. It's okay to turn it all the way off now. Can you tell us—were you a patient here?
  » Lights up.

- ME: Thank you. It's okay to turn it back off, okay. Can you turn it back off for me please?
  » Light turns off.

- ME: Thank you. Are you one of the suicides?
  » Lights up.

- Me (mumbling to Sam): That's why he's stuck here. He killed himself, he's stuck here.

- ME: Okay, turn it back off for me. You've almost got it. It's okay, turn it back off. ***At this point, the left light lights up, and the middle one had previously been the only one lighting up.***

- ME: Wow! That's really cool! Thank you for doing that, that's pretty awesome. You got me. I liked that so much I want to see it again. Can you concentrate and do it again? ***Does it again!***

- Video fades out.

After further review, this session made us think that we were speaking to a former female patient who had committed suicide and was now stuck. She didn't know how long she had been stuck, but it felt like a long time. She was not chased away by the noise of other people coming close to the room, and she lit up another flashlight on command.

We had a great time at St. Albans, and while we would be hard-pressed to play favorites, I think we agree that it was our favorite investigation that we've been on—both private and public hunts! We had a lot of stuff happen to us that we never would have expected. The visit blew us away.

Hydrotherapy. Not exactly a health spa. Patients would
be strapped inside an ice-cold tub to help calm them.

Where the females were locked down.
Sam captured an EVP here that says, "I'm here."

If You Decide to Visit:

Location & Contact Info

6248 University Park Drive
Radford, VA 24141
Tel: 540-260-3111

Email: *info@stalbans-virginia.com*

Contact: Jessica Wright—administrator and member of Mountain
Ridge Paranormal Research Society

Website

http://stalbans-virginia.com

Type of Tours/Hunts Offered

Private and public.

Haunted attraction for Halloween? Yes

Bathroom facilities? Port-a-potties. Indoor facilities are in the works.

Safe room for sleeping/snacking? More for snacking and resting.

Price: Catch them for specials when they run public events; $750.00
  private investigations for ten people.

Tips: The bowling alley seems to be the most popular place to hunt.
  Stake your claim early!

Closest airports: Roanoke Regional Airport—36 miles away; Raleigh-
  Durham International Airport—131 miles away; and Charlotte/
  Douglas International Airport—134 miles away.

Media Appearances

Resident Undead—Spring 2012

Sam's Observations

Ghost Face Thriller

St. Albans holds a special place with me. There were some firsts that happened there. It was the first time that I got massive chills associated with the paranormal. It was the first place where Jamie and I believed that we heard a disembodied voice at the same time. It's also where I first laid my eyes on a genuine apparition.

It was getting late into our ghost hunt. Jamie and I decided we'd stay one more hour before heading back to our hotel. We wanted to spend our time back at the Suicide Room, as we had had some odd experiences there earlier in the evening. As we walked up the stairs, we ran into Barry. He told us that "Red Eyes" (the name of an apparition known to haunt St. Albans) had recently been seen in the area. This excited both Jamie and me.

There was a small group (less than a dozen people) gathered in the main area, right below the stairs to the attic, listening as Chuck demonstrated how to use dowsing rods. Jamie and I stood in the background and observed. After a few minutes, someone in the group stated, "I just saw something move down the hallway!" Of course, everyone stopped what they were doing and looked down the hallway.

Two MRPRS members went down to investigate. They started to experience cold spots and asked for a volunteer to join them. Before they got the words out of their mouths, I was already down the hallway with them. It did seem a little colder in that specific area, but it didn't seem out of the ordinary. Other people started to fill up the hallway, looking for this Red Eyes character. After ten to fifteen minutes of searching the hallway (which is pretty much a small wing off the main room, with smaller rooms lined up on either side), everyone gathered back in the main area.

There was excitement in the air as everyone spoke of what had just happened and about their other experiences from earlier in the evening. I, on the other hand, quietly kept my focus on that hallway. The hallway was close to being pitch black, but I stared intently down it anyway. I wanted to see whatever had just caused all the commotion. Then it happened.

My eyes saw it before my brain realized what they were seeing. A whitish-gray face manifested about fifteen feet down the hallway from where I was standing! It was midway between the floor and ceiling. Its eye sockets and nostrils were black. It soon realized that I was "seeing" it, and it lurched back and quickly dissipated. A few seconds later, I saw it again as it came out of one of the rooms at the far end of the hallway. It looked at me again and then went back into that room.

Jamie was standing next to me, but she was facing the opposite direction listening to some other conversations. I grabbed her arm and quietly whispered in her ear, "I just saw something looking at us—a ghost's face." Her eyes widened as she said, "Are you serious?" I was serious. I kept it between the two of us because I didn't want my experience tainted by people that I did not know. I didn't want the power of suggestion to move through a room full of people and escalate to a point in which others might join in and say, "I saw it, too!" when they didn't.

I walked down the hallway, and there was no one down there or in any of the rooms. Once the crowd began to disband, Jamie and I spoke with members of MRPRS and told them what I saw. They confirmed to us that there had been previous apparition sightings in that area.

It's still hard for me to wrap my head around what I saw. It wasn't an illusion or a trick of the light. There was a definite contrast between the face and the surrounding darkness. It had no red eyes, though.

FOUR

TRANS-ALLEGHENY LUNATIC ASYLUM— WESTON, WEST VIRGINIA

Anyone interested in the history of this hospital should read *Weston State Hospital* by Kim Jacks. The Trans-Allegheny Lunatic Asylum was authorized in the 1850s and opened in the fall of 1864 (under the name West Virginia Hospital for the Insane to reflect the area's status as a new state) and was designed to follow the Kirkbride Plan. It was built for 250 patients. This was the era of moral treatment. The patient was to be provided comfortable living quarters and was to be nurtured. The Kirkbride Plan provided one attendant per six patients, and even violent patients weren't restrained unless they were suicidal.

Trans-Allegheny Lunatic Asylum.

Ms. Jacks recounts a description of the hospital's patients in 1871 on page 24:

> *Like all other institutions of this kind, the Asylum at Weston had its celebrities. One old man thinks himself the Creator of the Universe and delivers orations and toasts that are wonderful for their pomposity and extravagant incoherence. He attempted to prove to Governor Jacob and the Board of Directors and the visitors who were present last Thursday that the elephant is the greatest and first of all Gods, and he summoned the turtle as his witness. Another man has two ribs which he says belonged to the body of Adam. He carries them with him, tied by a leather thong. Another insists that he is dead and is importunate in his demand to be burned up. He says he has to be burned up some time, and it might as well be done at once ... Another spends his time in drawing pictures, beside which the sketches of horses, dogs, and houses delight idle urchins at school and are gems*

of fine art. A woman about forty years of age imagines herself a baby of about six months and cries and bawls to perfection. Some of the patients are suicidal and have to be carefully watched; others are homicidal and have to be restrained; but a large majority of them are peaceably disposed but are utterly incapable of taking care of themselves. Many of them, however, may work under direction of the attendants, and accordingly they are employed upon the farm and in many occupations about the house. The women do plain sewing and knitting; the men assist in the laundry, bake-house, carpenter shop, quarry, etc. One of the patients, who was for a number of years insane, and still has periods of occasional insanity, has made, with his own hands, nearly all of the finer furniture in the office and rooms of the Superintendent and other officers. The furniture is very beautiful in design and is very skillfully and substantially made.

By 1880, the hospital was already overcrowded, housing 491 patients. And because of the overcrowding situation experienced at institutions throughout the country, by the early 1900s, most hospitals had no choice but to abandon the moral treatment philosophy and become merely custodians of the patients. Restraints were in wide use now. This was the era of custodial care, during which state asylums became dumping grounds.

In 1915, the name of the hospital was changed again, this time to Weston State Hospital. As an example of just how horrible the overcrowding was, when a female patient died in 1927, the investigation turned up these staggering facts: there were only three attendants for every sixty-five patients and only three doctors for 1,300 patients.

Some of the treatments that patients received here included hydrotherapy, electroshock therapy, and even lobotomies. Hydrotherapy sounds innocuous enough. It isn't. Basically, a patient could remain in an ice-cold bathtub for days, all in the belief that it would induce fatigue. Depressed? They would blast you with what they called a "needle shower," which involved battering a patient with pressurized water (up to forty pounds per square inch) that was as cold as fifty degrees Fahrenheit. The 1940s and 1950s brought around shock treatments and prefrontal lobotomies (which were performed at hospitals across the United states, including at Weston). Dr. Freeman later developed the transorbital lobotomy, a simplified method. How progressive of him, since the prefrontal lobotomy involved drilling holes into the skull. He developed a way to render patients zombies by just knocking them unconscious with electroshock and then inserting an ice pick (essentially, from the looks of it) into their eyes and just sort of wiggling it around back and forth until he thought he had damaged the nerve fibers in the brain enough. Thank goodness Thorazine came along and made lobotomies obsolete.

By 1951, patient population had risen to 2,319, and finally fell to 1,500 by 1972. There were about 1,000 patients in the hospital in 1976.

In the late 1980s and early 1990s, several suicides and murders made the news, and Weston was arguably out of control. By 1994, the hospital was closed.

Events Leading up to the Hospital's Closure

Reports of problems at the hospital were plentiful in the news. One 1985 article in the *Charleston Gazette* reported the findings of a court-appointed monitor's three-day inspection, which was not good. Among other things, Weston Hospital was determined to be "dirty and unkempt," and some patients were even found naked and "confined to dirty wards with bathrooms smeared with feces."

Yet another *Charleston Gazette* article reported on horrible conditions in 1992. George Edward Bodie was a patient who died in a fight with another patient, David Michael Mason, who had murder charges brought against him five years previously. Brian Scott Bee was a patient whose badly decomposed body was found after eight days of being missing. His death was thought to be a suicide.

Our Experiences—April 14, 2012
Afternoon Civil War Tour and
Public Investigation—9:00 p.m.–5:00 a.m.

Have you ever had a building call out to you? The moment I laid eyes on this building, I knew I belonged there. I was drawn to it. Now I don't know what that says about me, since it was an insane asylum, but it was a magnet for me. The sight of it made me stop breathing and made my heart beat faster from the excitement and anticipation of what I knew was to come later that day and night as we explored the building. We arrived just in time to catch the last day tour—the first-floor tour. Our guide was dressed in an 1800s period costume. This was a great history tour that also provided ample opportunities to take photographs. We were told this is the oldest part of the building, dating back to the Civil War. During the day, you can better appreciate the sheer size of this campus. To the left of the main building, the TB hospital stands. The Medical Center (where we were told all of the lobotomies were performed) sits behind the main building, and the forensic building is to the right of the Medical Center. We did not see any entrances to the rumored tunnels while on the tour and forgot to ask about them until we had already left the property.

Fire door in Civil War Wing.

Hallway in the Civil War Wing, the oldest part of the building.

A shot from the sidewalk outside Trans-Allegheny.
I am in love with the aesthetics of this building.

Our favorite part of the tour was probably exploring the museum at the end. They have really done an impressive job creating exhibits related to the history of mental illness and how it was treated. The patient art gallery was stunning. I discovered an anonymous poem there that really struck me:

The Sly Man
I found that people did not have any souls
I couldn't get them back in class
I went to the sly man
He bought me coffee and told me of synchronicity
He said "I can be at two, three, or more places
At the same time"—you do not talk
He also said if it's proof of one or two things
That he would be back
If I talked—I would be back

We LOVED the check-in process for this investigation! In the lobby were three computer stations to check yourself in. So efficient! We were led through the first hallway on the right to the break room. A staff member called us out by name and gave us our personalized Certificates of Committal. This was a really fun touch and also a great souvenir. Then we were broken into groups of ten, and a guide was assigned to take us through the floors and rotate us. This worked very well.

One thing to note is that you will only have access to the main building. Not to worry—there is more than plenty to explore in this 242,000-square-foot building.

Second Floor—Ward 2

One of the big hotspots on this floor is a bathroom where a male patient made an advance on another male patient—and wound up getting stabbed seventeen times. Our guide recounted the horrifying tale of the patient trying to drag himself from the urinals all the way down the hallway to the nurse's station, but he never made it. Another tour guide claimed to have seen an apparition of a man leaning over the sink one night during a tour she was giving around Halloween!

In another room on this floor, a male patient hung himself from wrought iron curtain supports. There have been countless EVPs collected here that tell people to "get out," K2 hits, and flashlight activity.

The children's ward was also on this floor. One of the guides had a spirit box and felt something touch his arm. He then heard from the box: "I did."

Ward B was a female ward. There have been reports of doors slamming and random hits on the K2. Our guide told us that he has seen grown men run out of this ward because footsteps were coming toward them, and that he has seen things walking around the end of the hallway. (Note: The catwalk that goes around to the cafeteria can be found here, but it is locked because it is in such bad shape.)

I was drawn to a room on Ward B, so that is where we made our first stop after the tour of the second floor.

The door outside the isolation room, where the most
uncontrollable patients were sent to calm down. Some were
said to have been shackled to the floor of the bare space.

Second Floor—Isolation Room, Ward B/
Where We Meet Our Soldier Who Throws Gravel

Isolation rooms were considered hotspots because only the most disturbed patients (possibly criminally insane) ended up here. We got very lucky right away and captured a fantastic flashlight session on video. This is still one of my favorite experiences. We believe we were speaking with a Civil War soldier—he seemed to confirm his identity twice. We tried to get him to say his name in the voice recorder and believe that he said "Captain." (If you listen to the session clip, it sounds like he has a heavy foreign accent.) There are many reports of a Civil War soldier named Jacob who haunts the hospital. Maybe we were speaking with him. Here is an excerpt from the transcript of the session:

- ME: We're listening. It's just hard for us to hear you. But we've got a voice recorder down here and it's next to that gray box, so if you want to talk, talk into that and we'll get home and we'll play it and we'll try to hear you. Okay, how we'd like to talk to you with the flashlights is, we'll ask a question and if your answer is yes, that's when you turn the light on. **Okay, so you can jump in anytime.**
  » Lights up.

- ME: Okay. That must mean you're male. Are we talking to a man or a boy? I'm starting to think something's wrong with my flashlight.

- SAM: Can you please turn one of those lights on again for us? We thank you for doing it.
  » Lights up.

- SAM: Can you turn that light on if you were a patient here?

• SAM: Can you turn that light on if you were part of the staff here?

• ME: If you weren't a patient here and you didn't work here, does that mean that you were here before this hospital was here? Turn the light on if that's right.

• ME: Okay, different question. Maybe you don't know anymore. Are you not sure?

» Lights up.

• ME: Okay, dial it back down for me. I want to try to figure something else out. Are you stuck here? Are you stuck in this building, or on this land, or even in this room? Do you feel like you can't leave from this place—is that what's going on?

• ME: Different question. Do you like it here?

• SAM: Can you turn that light on if you fought in the Civil War?

» Lights up.

• SAM: Thank you.

• ME: Did you die here on this land or close to here? Can you tell me if you're not sure?

• ME: Can you just confirm for us again—and I'm sorry to ask you again, but can you just confirm for us again that you did fight in the Civil War—that you were a soldier? Can you light it up if that's right?

» Lights up.

- ME: Thank you. You don't understand how important that just was. You just confirmed for us [EVP captured: "**Say what?**"] that you fought in the Civil War!

- SAM: Can you please turn that off? I've got another question to ask. Please light it up if I hit on the correct one.

- SAM: Are you from Europe?
  » Lights up.

- ME: You came to America on a ship. You came across the ocean to get to this country? Is that a yes?
  » Lights up.

- ME: I hope that you're telling us your name in that recorder because I really want to know who you are. The recorder is in the corner. I'm going to be quiet for thirty seconds. Just go over there and say your name. We'll hear it when we get home. Okay. (EVP captured sounds like "**Captain.**") I will listen to that later because I want to know who you are.

- SAM: Both Jamie and my family came from Scotland and Ireland. Pretty much a lot of people where we live came from there. Her last name is Davis.
  » Lights up.

- ME: It's so nice to talk to you. If you want to, you can turn it back off and we'll keep asking you questions. It's amazing.
  » Light turns off.

- ME: Okay, thank you.

- ME: Can you see us? I know you can hear us, but can you see us?
  » Lights up.

- ME: How come we can't see you?

- SAM: Can you show yourself to us? I promise we won't do anything to you if you do. We'll stay right over here in this corner.

- ME: I can't see you yet if you're trying.
  » Lights up.

- ME (to Sam): I think that means he's trying.

- ME: That's okay. I don't know if I was ready for that. I don't know if you understand. Can you turn the light on if you know why you're still here?

- ME (to Sam): Something just made a noise down here. Did you just make that noise?
  » Lights up.

- ME: Did you just throw a rock at me?

- ME: Do you talk to people who come in here a lot?
  » Lights up.

This was just such an amazing conversation for me. This was one of those times where I could actually feel this guy's spirit. I could tell that he was in the room with us. While I felt that he was friendly and maybe a little mischievous, I still wasn't really prepared to actually see what he would look like if he were able to manifest. I believe we were legitimately speaking with a Civil War soldier who came to America on a ship from Europe. He seemed to indicate that he talks to people at Trans-Allegheny a lot, that he could see us, and that he believed in God before he died.

Sam reminded me to point out that he did a sweep of this room with the K2 before we began our investigation. He got a very strong red-line reading in one corner. He thought he was getting a false positive, so he dismissed it and began setting up our equipment. After our flashlight session, he did another K2 sweep. This time, the K2 did not register anything! Combine this with the flashlight video and the rock being thrown at me (this WAS NOT something that fell from the ceiling), and we were experiencing a ton of activity all at once!

Third Floor

Our guide told us that this was the most feared floor by workers when the hospital was still open. We were told that a girl actually lit herself on fire up here. Our guide also told us that he has seen a male apparition just sitting on the floor in a room. Another time, he was giving a tour and one group broke off to go to the opposite end of the floor. The group he was with heard them screaming. But when they all moved to find out what the screaming was all about, the other group thought that THEY had been the ones screaming! He also told us that the only time he had ever been scared in the building was on the third floor when something was stomping up to him. He couldn't see a thing, and it stopped right before it got all the way to him. Copperhead (another one of the guides) has had one of his flashlights melt, and he says that someone who goes by the name of "Big John" is up here.

Our guide told us about Tom, an orderly who knows that he is dead, still loves his coffee, and if he likes you, well...he will follow you around and kind of watch over you. Lily is another one that seems to like the third floor, and people say they talk to her to all the time.

If you were a violent male patient,
you were locked away up here on the third floor.

Our last stop was in Dean's room. Our guide told us the heartbreaking story of a patient being murdered by two other men. When their attempts to hang him failed, they beat his head in with the leg from a bed. When asked what happened, employees were told by the murderers that Dean "was breathing too much oxygen." Now, a lot of times, stories such as this simply cannot be corroborated through news articles or other forms of publicly accessible records. What you have is a retelling of an event from workers, emergency responders, or other various firsthand sources that gets modified as it is passed down, getting farther and farther away from the truth (as you know such stories have a tendency to do).

But in this case, what happened to Dean was horrifyingly real. See the below article titled "Competency Tests Ordered for Patients":

The Charleston Gazette
Saturday, November 8, 1987

WESTON (UPI) A Lewis County judge has ordered two severely ill mental patients accused of murdering another patient at Weston Hospital to undergo competency tests.

Lewis County Circuit Judge Thomas Keadle issued the order Thursday on David Mason, 25, and James Woods, 30, county prosecutor Harold Bailey said.

They were charged Tuesday with first-degree murder and malicious wounding by a Lewis County grand jury. They are accused of killing Dean Metheny, 49, in an all-male unit of the mental hospital Sept. 17.

An autopsy showed the victim died of breathing blood into the lungs, which is similar to drowning. Deputy Medical Examiner Kirk Griffith said Metheny had many broken bones on his face, bruises on the face and neck, broken ribs, and a lacerated liver.

Another court hearing is scheduled Nov. 16, Bailey said. He said Keadle wants psychiatrists to determine if the suspects are competent to stand trial and understand criminal responsibility.

"Just because you're in a mental hospital doesn't mean you don't know right from wrong," Bailey said.

On page 122 of *Weston State Hospital*, Kim Jacks recalls interviewing Dr. Todt about his first meeting with one of the men who murdered Dean and most likely another patient:

The first day I walked up on the unit with the Medical Director, and the guy walked up to me and looked at me with his Hannibal Lector eyes and said, "I'm gonna cut your heart out."

Third Floor—Ward F, Violent Men's Ward/"Dean's Room"

After our guide showed us around the third floor, we stayed behind in what is known as "Dean's room." We were almost immediately rewarded with activity, although, admittedly, some of it did not seem to be in response to our questions, or the answers seemed contradictory. For instance, on two occasions, the entity seemed to indicate with the flashlights that it was the same soldier that we were speaking with earlier in the evening but then indicated that it was someone else entirely. Our impression of this session was that either we were speaking with someone who was having difficulty being responsive or we were running on some kind of delay. The transcript of our flashlight session is as follows:

- ME: Don't let that camera scare you. Sam's just trying to get that light on tape. I think you're trying to tell us that you're here. We won't go away if you're trying to talk to us. Is that right?
  » Left flashlight and then the middle one light up. (Sam missed it on camera, but I saw it.)

- ME: If you want us to stay and talk to you, can you turn that light on so we'll know that you want us to stay?

- SAM: Do you want us to leave? Turn on the light.

- ME: If you want us to leave we will—just turn the light on and we'll go. Where'd you go? Are you still here? You've got to tell us or we're going to leave. All right. There's nothing going on here. False alarm.
  » Lights up.

- ME: How about the light on the far left? Can you turn that one on? All right, you've got my attention.

- ME: Do you want to tell me something else? Are you the same soldier that I was talking to earlier tonight? Can you turn the light on if this is you again?
  » Left flashlight and then the middle one light up again.

- ME: Two at the same time?! You're just showing off! Are you showing off for me? Maybe a little bit?
  » Middle one lights up.

- ME: Let me tell you something. Not everybody can turn both of these lights on at the same time. I've actually only seen it happen one other time. Well, show off some more! Can you do it some more for me?
  » Middle one lights up.

- ME: I like it. Do both of them. Please can you do both of them? I'll count to ten. Don't do anything until I get to ten, and then see if you can turn both those lights on for me. (I get to ten and nothing happens.)

- ME: What happened? Did you go away? I thought you were going to do something when I got to ten. Can you turn the light on if you're here alone?
  » Middle one lights up.

- ME: Were you a patient here?
  » Left flashlight lights up.

- ME: If you were a patient here can you turn the middle light on?

- ME: Well did you use to work here?

- ME: I'm kind of starting to think I'm talking to my soldier again. Am I talking to my soldier?
  » Middle one lights up.

- ME: All right, if I'm talking to my soldier again, I want to see that light in the far left go off. Did you follow me up here from the third floor? (Nothing happens.)

- ME: That means I'm talking to someone else. Is that right?
  » Middle one lights up.

- ME: You haven't talked to me until now.
  » Left flashlight and then the middle one light up again.

- ME (to Sam): See, that's something. With the different lights going off. That's something. It's just playing with it!

- SAM: Can you turn that third one on? The one that hasn't been turned on yet? Can you make the gray box light up with the green light? You still in here with us?

- ME: I can't remember if you were in here or not, but if your answer to a question is "yes," that's when you turn the light on.
  » Middle one lights up.

- ME: I don't know what that means. I didn't ask a question.

Sometimes we come across something that just maybe seems as though they want to play with the lights and are not necessarily responding to us or even trying to interact with us. This seemed like a mix of both. First, he indicated that I was talking to my soldier from earlier—again—and then he indicated he was someone else. It was still significant to us to see the manipulation of different flashlights simultaneously, and it did seem as though he was trying to show off a little bit and keep our attention. Perhaps we came across a ghost with a very short attention span, or maybe we were speaking with someone who was mentally disabled.

The next stop we made was to explore the Doctor's Quarters (which has been decorated in period-specific furniture).

At this point, I trekked back downstairs by myself for a bathroom break and left Sam to his own devices. With his voice recorder on, he announced to the empty room: "Is there anybody here with me tonight? I'm solo right now. Jamie went to the restroom." There was no immediate reaction, but later on when reviewing for EVPs, something responded, **"Oh, I should have known."** We think that is just hilarious!

The Doctor's Quarters. The owners have accurately re-created the look of this room, but these are not the original furnishings.

Fourth Floor

This was originally where the employees lived. This floor was turned into a drug and alcohol ward. Our guide told us that there are two spirits named Frank and Larry who seem to be around a lot. He has seen things pop their heads out of rooms and said that there is usually something going on up here. "At times," the guide said, "it sounds like there is a party going on up here." If you ask me, that sounds perfectly fitting for a drug and alcohol ward.

FOURTH FLOOR, WARD R—DEMON HALLWAY?

To me, this was the creepiest part of the whole hospital. I felt completely at ease everywhere else, but something about this area really gave me the hee-bie-jeebies. To be fair, our guide did say that he had some personal experiences up here with something that seemed like a nonhuman entity. But I was already creeped out! The story we heard was that one of the guides had a group up here, and they were going through a flashlight session with a group of people—"Are you a man? Are you a woman? Are you a child?"—and nothing was getting a hit. Then someone asked, "Are you something else?" The flashlight lit right up! Two other members of the group had split off to explore elsewhere on the floor because they were more experienced and wanted to conduct their own sessions. When they came back to the guide and the rest of the group, they showed a video that they had captured of a light darting out of a door and then their spirit box saying, "Demon." From what I have heard, there were plenty of patients who thought they were all kinds of things—royalty, politicians, you name it. So maybe one is still around trying to scare people by claiming to be a demon. Or hell, maybe it really was a demon. I don't know. Who knows what it was?

We stayed up there with our guide and did a flashlight session using his flashlight and our three flashlights. We sat them all upright this time, so the light would be pointing at the ceiling. For some reason, we could not get anything to interact with us using our own flashlights, but whatever was there was quite responsive to our guide's request! I almost got the feeling that we were being snubbed—like whoever was up there trying to communicate didn't know us and didn't want to know us, but he knew our guide and was comfortable interacting with him.

I did not want to leave, but by this time of the night, I was absolutely drained, so I begged Sam to take me away, promising that we would return soon.

Trans-Allegheny is very much a museum and showplace, and we think that it would be an interesting visit for anyone, not just those interested in the paranormal field. It is truly a fascinating place.

Another one of the scariest hallways
in the world to walk down alone in the dark.

Vintage wheelchair.

If You Decide to Visit:

Location & Contact Info

71 Asylum Drive

Weston, WV 26452

Tel: 304-269-5070

Fax: 304-269-5071

Email: *info@trans-alleghenylunaticasylum.com*

Website

www.talawv.com

Type of Tours/Hunts Offered

Private and public hunts; historic and civil war tours, festivals.

Haunted attraction for Halloween? Yes

Bathroom facilities? Yes

Safe room for sleeping/snacking? More for snacking.

Size: 242,000 sq. ft. of main building to explore.

Price: $100 for public hunts; $150 per person for private hunts (minimum ten people).

Tips: Get there early enough to go on the tour of all the floors and allow time at the end to explore the museum sections!

Closest airports: Pittsburgh International Airport—101 miles away; Port Columbus International Airport—146 miles away; and Washington Dulles International Airport—162 miles away.

Media Appearances

Ghost Hunters, Season 4, Episode 409—4/30/08

Ghost Adventures Live, Episode 1—10/30/09

Ghost Hunters Academy—6/9/10

Paranormal Challenge—7/29/11

Sam's Observations

Trans-Allegheny is right up with Waverly Hills when it comes to paranormal clout. All of the top ghost hunting groups in the country have investigated here. This insane asylum did not disappoint us!

The very first place that we investigated here was a small isolation room. Jamie had mentioned to me during our tour that this is where she wanted to start. She is usually spot on when it comes to choosing areas to investigate. I believe that she is more in tune with the paranormal than I am. I believe that it's something that runs in her family.

I started our investigation with a K2 sweep of the room. I got a very strong, red-line reading in one particular area. So strong, in fact, that I thought we were getting one of the "false positives" that our guide told us are in the building. I dismissed the reading and went ahead with setting up our equipment.

After we completed our amazing flashlight session with the Civil War spirit, I did another K2 sweep. I got nothing. Not even one blip! What I had originally dismissed as some sort of electrical current in the room now became another piece of evidence. To me, this further validated that Jamie and I were not alone in there.

Combine the K2 readings, the flashlight session, the EVPs that were captured, as well as that rock being tossed at Jamie, and to date, this was the most activity that we experienced in one confined area.

Contrary to what you might think, you can get evidence in a public hunt.

FIVE

YORKTOWN HOSPITAL— YORKTOWN, TEXAS

The Felician Sisters of the Roman Catholic Church founded Yorktown Hospital in 1950. The hospital closed in the late 1980s and was briefly turned into a drug rehabilitation center. It is estimated that the hospital saw fifty deaths per year, which is a total of about 2,000 during its history.

While death was a common occurrence, two have garnered special attention—a possible double homicide that took place in the basement, rumors of which have been retold on television and throughout the Internet. You can still see what is said to be the bloodstained wall where it occurred. The story goes that a female staff member was involved with two male patients. One day, she was caught by one of the males, who observed her speaking quietly with the other. He flew into a rage and stabbed them both to death. Is it true? A records request to the police department turned up absolutely nothing. However, because so much time has passed, it is unlikely that responsive records could have been produced even if they did exist at one time. The same thing goes for corroborating the sad story of T. J. He was allegedly dropped off on the steps of the hospital by some friends late one night. No one rang the bell for help. The nuns found him in the morning, dead of a heroin overdose.

Yorktown Hospital.

Our Experiences—April 20, 2012 Private Investigation—4:00 p.m.–2:00 a.m.

Mike got us checked in, and we spent the afternoon exploring the hospital, taking photos, and sitting in the chapel.

Before he left us on our own, Mike gave us some parting words of advice: don't run from anything in this building. And also, if you get into an area where you can't breathe or you feel someone is pressing on your chest or choking you, just walk back about fifty feet away, right away, and the feeling should leave you. Don't try to ride it out because the nausea will stick with you.

During the daytime, I felt a little uneasy walking around the hospital, even with Sam there with me. Certain places here plunge you into darkness—crevices of the building, I guess. Areas that you sort of find yourself getting lost in, maybe. The only way I can explain the feel of it is to tell you to go there yourself. But please listen to me now when I tell you this: the place is straight out of a horror movie. I found my imagination running amok on more than one occasion. This hospital is the scariest place I have ever been. Very shortly, I became obsessed with the fact that a killer was hiding out in the hospital waiting for us. Sam told me I was being ridiculous.

Mike had just gotten back from the lumberyard and was doing some repairs out back. All I knew was that I heard the sound of sawing and hammering but could not see Mike. I then became obsessed with the idea that Mike was out back building our coffins. And that as soon as it got dark, Mike was going to enter the hospital and stalk and murder us. (No offense, Mike. We thought you were a really nice guy, but I'm sure you can understand how easy it is for one's imagination to run wild.) Once again, Sam told me I was being ridiculous. But I saw him cut his eyes in a certain way that indicates he is seriously taking my concerns to heart. I had struck a nerve, and he was legitimately trying to weigh the chances of us being murdered at Yorktown.

Some of the paranormal phenomena reported here includes a full-body apparition seen outside the chapel, red glowing eyes, phantom organ music, and people feeling as though they are being choked.

The chapel does have an old organ that flat out gave me the creeps. When I got home, I searched online about it, and there is a rumor on the Internet that it belonged to a serial killer. I asked the owner, Phil Ross, if he knew anything about the piano, and he referred me to Jo Ann Marks-Rivera of the Black Swan Inn in San Antonio, the owner of the organ. She told me she purchased the organ from an estate sale. She later learned from the estate's caretaker that the previous owner had picked up a man and brought him home with him for a few days. After a night of partying, the homeowner did not come down for breakfast, so the caretaker went up to his room. The caretaker found his boss murdered in his bed—his head had been bashed in and the unknown guest was long gone.

Ms. Marks-Rivera is quoted in an article titled "Group Set to Capitalize on Apparitions at Yorktown Hospital" about her impressions of spirits at Yorktown:

> *Hauntings are typically expressions of the way the people died, that most are only trying to express themselves in their states of unrest. Of a trip to Yorktown, Marks-Rivera said: One of them kept telling us to get the f_ _ _ out of here, but when we talked to him we understood that he was trying to warn us. He had been butchered by a Dr. Nowierski during a thyroid operation and was trying to help us out, keep us safe.*

I like this quote because it points out that what you think is being threatening to you may in fact just be someone trying to warn you or communicate with you. Too often, the message gets lost in translation.

Just as a side note, the hospital has been "dressed" with all of the props that you will see. It is fun to explore and certainly adds to the ambiance, but these are not original items from when the hospital was open.

The chapel at Yorktown Hospital.

Basement—*The Shy Ghost*

When we started our investigation down here, it was actually still light outside. Whatever was down here would light up the K2 like crazy and utilize the flashlights, but as soon as Sam made a move to capture it on video, all activity would immediately stop. Sam would say, "Okay, I'll turn it off." And then within a few minutes, things would start lighting up once again. For the most part, the activity wasn't responsive to us—it seemed as though someone was just playing with our tools and trying them out.

This place has been nicknamed "EVP Hospital," and we found out why when we got home. While we were in the basement hallway, I asked, "Are we talking to a kid?" And in return, we received a very loud yell, "NO!" We did not hear it at the time, so we think we can rule out the possibility of the voice being a kid playing near the hospital.

After spending about an hour in the basement, we announced that we were packing up and moving to the main floor. The K2 was going nuts upon my announcing this—lighting up all the way to red. From this point forward, I felt as though someone was following me. And not just to communicate with me. The feeling was that something wanted to sort of harass me or have a little bit of fun with me.

Imagine my shock when we got home and Sam played some EVPs for me:

- SAM: Will you turn one of the flashlights on?
  » UNKNOWN MALE: **Yes.**

- ME: Just for a minute, so we know there's nothing wrong with our K2.
  » UNKNOWN MALE: **It's hot in here.**
  » UNKNOWN FEMALE: **Jamie.**

- ME: We'd really like to talk to you, and the best way for us to do that is for us to ask you a question, and then you turn either the gray box—light it up, or to turn one of the flashlights on.
  » UNKNOWN FEMALE: **Jamie.**

- ME: Do you want to try it?

- SAM: I promise that I won't get a camera out while I'm down here anymore. Do you feel more comfortable like that?
  » UNKNOWN FEMALE: **They want Jamie.**

What does she mean by "They want Jamie!?" *They want Jamie… WHAT?!?!?* This really creeps me out! Who is "they" for one thing? And are these spirits sitting around talking about me or plotting against me? Maybe the message was just that someone wanted to talk to me. I just don't know, but that is what I tell myself so I can sleep at night. Yeah, that's it. They just wanted to tell me something.

There is a room down here where the original jail cell from the old Yorktown Jail is. We had no idea what it was at the time we were down here. We were guessing maybe it was some type of drunk tank or a place for someone who had been arrested to wait before being processed. Mike filled us in later.

We headed back to the chapel around 9:00 p.m. We probably spent twenty or thirty minutes in there trying to make something happen, but nothing was going on. I just sat very still in one of the pews and tried not to breathe too much. We got back home, and dang if you don't hear the same female voice saying my name again in here!

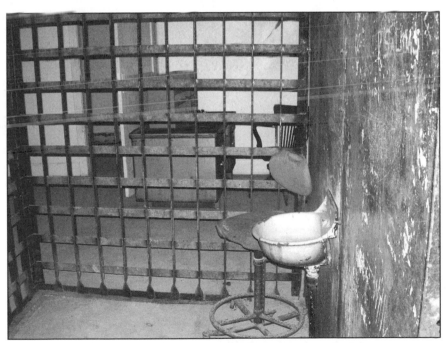

The original jail cell from Yorktown Jail. It looks out of place because the cell was not initially part of the hospital.

- SAM: Can somebody tell me what these big wicker appa-
ratuses are, on either side of the room, suspended from the
ceiling. Some sort of symbolism, but don't really know. I'm
not a Catholic. So I'm not real sure what they are.
  » UNKNOWN FEMALE: Moan.
  » UNKNOWN FEMALE: Jamie.

Main Floor—The Breather

We pulled a chair into the hallway and sat for a few minutes trying to do
a flashlight session. At this point, it was pitch black. I had pretty much
made up my mind to stop talking because I felt so threatened. I didn't
want to encourage any kind of interaction whatsoever. I froze in the chair,
sat as rigid as I could, and tried not to breathe too much. I was ready to
go. I kept feeling like someone was breathing in my left ear, and it was
making me feel very uncomfortable. I did not actually feel a breath but
just heard the sound of someone exhaling into my ear. And I hated it.
Sam asked me if I wanted to go upstairs. I didn't, but I went anyway.

Third Floor—The Trickster in the Library

After leaving the main hallway on the second floor, we went upstairs to
the sofa room. Once again, something followed me and was breathing
in my ear. I was so bothered and out of sorts that Sam led the flashlight
session, which is very unusual for me. We captured a Class A EVP up
here of what sounds to me like the same woman—and she says my name
again! So I was right. My feelings were very much picking up on something going on, even if I couldn't hear it or see it at the time. Something
was with me, and she was very much trying to get my attention. An
excerpt from the transcript reads:

- SAM: Are you someone that's just passing through here?
Can you please turn the light on?
  » Lights up.

• SAM: Can you turn it on if you're a male?

• SAM: What about a child?
  » Lights up.

• SAM: I see there's a ball out in the hallway. Can you roll that ball? It's right out in the doorway. Can you please roll that ball for me? Can you hit it or kick it?
  » Lights up.

• SAM: It would be a really neat thing (**Lights up.**) if you want to kick it toward me, I'll kick it back to you. You want to try? Can you try? The light doesn't have to be on to move that ball. I can see it. Okay. So please kick that ball over there. Make it move. Roll it. If you can turn that flashlight on, I know you can move that ball. If you need to save up some energy, that's fine. I can wait.

• ME: Are you looking for your mom?
  » Lights up.

• SAM: What Jamie said, is that correct? Are you lost? Can you turn the light on if you're lost?

• SAM: So do you know where you are?

• SAM: Are you still here? Can you turn the light on if you're still here?
  » Lights up.

• SAM: Can you try to turn on one of the other flashlights?
  » Right one turns on again—the purple one, same one it has been using.

• SAM: What about one on the other side?

» Right one turns on again. EVP: "**Yes.**"

• ME: Can you tell me—did you just come into the hospital because you heard us ask if someone wanted to talk to us? Are you here because we're trying to talk to you? Is that why?

• ME: Are you here because you know somebody here? (I whisper to Sam that someone is breathing on me again. "This place is seriously messing with my head.")

» Lights up.

• ME: Somebody is breathing on me. And it's really irritating me. I don't like it, it was doing it to me downstairs.

• SAM: Don't get close to Jamie. Communicate through the K2 or the flashlights. Can you please try to turn on one of the other flashlights?

» Turns on right one again—the purple one, same one it has been using.

• SAM: Can you turn on the flashlight if you don't like it here? You wish you could leave?

» **Laughter is caught on recorder.**

• SAM: Are you still here with us?

» Lights up. EVP: "**I'm faint.**"

• ME: Are you really a kid? Are we really talking to a child? I thought you told us that you were a child earlier?

• SAM: Is that true?

• SAM: If it's not true, can you turn the light on?

» Lights up.

• SAM: All right, so you've been tricking us, huh?

• ME: I don't like that. I don't like the breathing, and I don't like the lies.

Yorktown's library. When investigating this area, we encountered something pretending to be a child.

I made Sam call Mike after this session to tell him we were leaving so he could lock up. Sam didn't want to go—it was only about 9:45—but I was done. I was convinced that something was following me around the place and breathing in my ear. I felt harassed, and it was really getting to me. I don't know if it was trying to scare me or just get my attention, but I had a gut feeling to leave that I just couldn't ignore any longer. It was time to go, whether Sam was ready or not. We cut our investigation way short because of the overwhelming feelings I was having. Did I just get scared and let my fear take over? Sure, this is possible, but I don't think this is what happened. I've gotten scared before. It has always been in connection with a specific area, and once I leave the area, the fear or bad feelings have always gone away. I had never experienced fear of the entire location like this—to the point that I'm convinced something is following me around. No, this was something else. Something that never happened before and hasn't happened anywhere else since. This was a game of cat and mouse, and I was the mouse. Something was preying on me or toying with me, and it wasn't a good feeling at all. I almost took it as a warning.

Before we left for the night, I told Mike about feeling like someone was breathing on me. He said he has experienced that, too. As for the upstairs room? He said there is a little girl up there who likes it when people read to her. He also told us a funny story about a guy who talked a little too much during his investigation. He was running through a flashlight session and asked, "Do you want us to leave?" Nothing happened. He then asked, "Do you want me to leave?" Two of the flashlights lit up. The guy said aloud, "I wonder why she wants me to leave?" A cute little girl voice then came over the recorder: "You talk too much."

I also asked Mike if he had ever witnessed anything in the hospital that scared him. He told us of a time where he was in the main hallway with his girlfriend and his dog, a German shepherd. He said that one night he saw something crawling very quickly toward him on the floor, and that while it was happening, he thought it was his dog running toward him. But when the shadow got closer to him, he actually saw the face of a woman. He said he would never forget her face.

The Aftermath

We were probably a good thirty miles out from Yorktown, headed back to the Menger in San Antonio to catch some sleep before our flight back to Atlanta when we remembered that we had forgotten something. We had forgotton to give our speech for when we are leaving. We forgot to tell everyone that they couldn't come with us. Sam quickly ran through our speech about nobody coming with us, and I tried to relax. But I had that sinking pit in my stomach telling me that we had messed up. Something was off. Nothing unusual happened my first night home (on Sunday evening).

On Monday night, I had gone to dinner with some friends after work and did not get back home until around 8:30 p.m. I immediately noticed that the hallway light for the stairs was on. I am usually very good at remembering to turn all of the lights off when I leave for work in the morning, but I do forget from time to time. So I noticed it, but I didn't really think anything of it.

I settled in, got myself ready for bed, and eventually fell asleep. I awoke in the middle of the night and opened my eyes to what can only be described as a real hag of an old woman. I only saw her for a split second, but she was right in my face. I wasn't paralyzed in bed by this. Instead I immediately jumped up in the dark and threw the bright lights on. Nothing was there; nothing was "off" or felt different in any way. I opened my bedroom door and noticed that the hallway light for the stairs was on again. Now I was pissed off and starting to get a little nervous (and maybe just downright scared). This never happens. The last thing I do before going to bed is turn that light off and look behind me into the darkness to make sure I got the kitchen light, too. I've never forgotten this light. NEVER EVER. So now I'm thinking that not only am I dealing with an old hag, but I'm also dealing with someone who is trying to make me incur additional expenses on my electric bill every month. And hell no, I just can't have that!

But I didn't say anything or acknowledge anything out loud. Just sort of a "hmph!" I flipped the lights back off and went back to bed. I didn't get too far into sleeping again before I was awakened by my upstairs fire alarms. I got my handy step stool out and unscrewed every single one of those suckers and took the batteries out.

I went back to sleep. The next night, I went and stayed with my parents. I told my dad everything that happened and how I was scared that I had brought something back from Yorktown since we had forgotten to say anything until we were already traveling. He told me I just had a nightmare. But he also told me that I needed to march back in my house the next day right after work and take my house back.

So I did. I walked in MY HOUSE, and I said, "I don't know if anyone is here. I don't know if you can hear me. But if you can, you have to leave. I can't help you. If you do anything here to try to get my attention, I will act like I don't see it, or hear it, or feel it. I will never acknowledge that you are real to me. And I absolutely WILL NEVER help you, anywhere, or under any circumstances. Go. Now. This is my house. You are not welcome here."

I have not had any trouble sleeping or any nightmares since. I have also not had any lights left on. And you better believe that Sam and I never again forgot to say our departing speech to deter any travelers from coming home with us.

Looking back, I question myself about how I handled this investigation. The sense that I got at the time was to keep my head down, be quiet, and not encourage whatever was trying to interact with me. Maybe I missed an opportunity to help someone, and I hate that. But I can only go with what I sense at the time. Perhaps there will come another time when I can return and try to listen out for that unknown female voice. I would like to know who she is and what she was trying to tell me.

An operating room on the second floor.

A supply cabinet in an examination room contains reference books,
medicine bottles, and a jar of teeth (second shelf on the left).

The pediatric unit.

If You Decide to Visit:

Location & Contact Info

728 West Main Street

Yorktown, TX 78164

Email: *yorktownhospital@live.com*

Owner: Phil Ross

Contact on site: Mike Henson

Website

http://yorktownhospital.com

Type of Tours/Hunts Offered

Not open to the general public—contact the owner to make a request.

Haunted attraction for Halloween? No

Bathroom facilities? No

Safe room for sleeping/snacking? No

Size: About 30,000 sq. ft.

Price: Contact Phil Ross.

Tips: One thing to bear in mind while doing your investigation is that you will be fighting the noise of the tractor trailers speeding by the hospital. This isn't a constant noise by any means, but in some areas it will be very loud. Dairy Queen is your bathroom stop. Call Mike the day before your hunt to confirm arrival time.

Closest airports: San Antonio International Airport—70 miles away; Corpus Christi International Airport—84 miles away; Austin-Bergstrom International Airport—84 miles away; and George Bush Intercontinental Airport—148 miles away.

Media Appearances

Ghost Adventures, Season 4, Episode 21—3/28/11

Stranded, Season 1, Episode 6—3/27/13

Yorktown—2011

Sam's Observations

Yorktown Hospital is by far the creepiest location that we visited. It's like something you would see in an apocalyptic movie—a hospital that's been abandoned, just sitting for years. There is even a full-size chapel attached to it. The chapel is still filled with pews, confessional booths, and a pulpit. All of it just sitting under dust.

We had a good investigation, don't get me wrong. We had flashlight responses, a disembodied yell (in the basement), and tons of EVPs. Jamie even felt as though something was following her around, breathing in her ear (and after listening to the voice-recorded evidence, something was definitely following her around). This place did deliver.

I should have prefaced these comments by saying that I have not been scared or have had any "bad" feelings about any of the places listed in this book. Now, if Yorktown Hospital was in a different setting, say off in a rural area surrounded by foliage with no other buildings in sight, I would have definitely had a very hard time walking into it!

SIX

FARRAR SCHOOL—
MAXWELL, IOWA

The Farrar school opened in 1922 and shut down in 2002. I could not find any records of events that would explain any haunting(s) in a conventional way—no sudden deaths or mysterious circumstances regarding anything or anyone. But I have come to believe that doesn't mean anything. In other words, I don't believe that someone has to die on a property to be able to visit it in death. I think some spirits wander around just like we breathing folks do. Some of us spend our lives traveling back to visit places that meant something to us, coupled with time spent exploring new destinations. Others just stay close to home and never see much or do much. I think spirits are just the same way. I don't know who, why, or what. But something (or some things, maybe) is in that schoolhouse.

Farrar School.

And apparently something was there before the school even closed. Several former students and employees have said that while school was in session, they experienced things like phantom footsteps, lights turning on and off by themselves, and doors that seem to slam shut on their own. During renovations, workers reported hearing children's voices.

The current owners have had several personal experiences, and I am including an excerpt from an article from the *Des Moines Register* to speak more to that:

Des Moines Register—Des Moines, Iowa
October 18, 2010
By Melanie Lageschulte

Nancy Oliver sometimes had dreams in which she lived in a spacious building that sported a stage. Those came true in late 2006 when she and her husband, Jim, purchased the three-story, 17,000-square-foot school in this rural Polk County community.

The school had been shuttered since 2002, but the couple quickly settled into their living quarters on the first floor and began renovations.

Then the odd experiences started:

A voice reminding Nancy Oliver to turn off the bathroom light.

A steadying hand on her shoulder while she was climbing one of the school's several stairwells.

The shadowy shape of a little boy on the gymnasium stairs.

Things just got weirder when a psychic, Jacqui Carpenter of nearby Maxwell, pulled into the drive and asked if she could communicate with a ghost she said was inside.

"I've always felt very comfortable here," Nancy Oliver said, but it's a good thing she and her husband are a bit skeptical.

"We really need to be, or we'd just be seeing things right and left."

During a recent investigation, Carpenter and grandson Austin Cory crouched on the floor of a former classroom as other researchers sat nearby in a handful of student desks.

Carpenter said she sensed a girl was present—and then another spirit she referred to as Frank, who apparently liked to steal the show during past investigations.

"Let the little girl come forward," Carpenter said.

She asked the spirit if it would answer some questions by lighting up an electromagnetic sensor. Carpenter asked the spirit if it was a male and got no response. When she asked if it was female, the reader's red light glowed.

Then she told the spirit she wanted to know its age. Carpenter started counting at six and slowly ticked off numbers until she reached 10, when the red light began to flash repeatedly.

Carpenter said the apparent interaction with the girl was interesting but she couldn't accept it without some other evidence. "This is fun, but we don't know what we're messing with," she said.

Our Experiences—May 6, 2012: Private Investigation

The schoolhouse is not quite in the middle of nowhere, but it is pretty close to it. A beautiful, Iowa farmland kind of nowhere. One that goes from sweet-smelling, clean air to cow smell in the blink of an eye. We loved it. We both said we could pack up and move to Iowa in a second! Nancy met us and gave us a tour of the school.

Gym and Boiler Room

We started out in the boiler room and got some flashlight and K2 activity going on. Just like at Yorktown, though, every time Sam turned the camera on, the activity would stop! We were twelve minutes into our session when I said, "All right, nothing is happening, we're going to go." And the flashlight turned itself on! Sam turned the camera on to capture the session, and then nothing else would happen. He said, "Okay, if you're shy, I'll turn this camera off. We would rather communicate with you than capture a video." And he turned the camera off. And lo and behold, the flashlight lit right back up!

The gym was a creepy-feeling place to be. It is almost as if you can feel the residual energy still down there. We observed the K2 lighting up several times while we were sitting at the table down there.

Nancy shared her personal experience of an encounter on the stairwell that leads down to the gym. While on her way down, she saw a boy who was on his way up the stairs. It was 11:00 a.m. and the light was on. He appeared as a black shadow that was about three and a half feet tall, with one foot in front of him on the stair and the other foot on the stair behind him. She watched him for a couple of seconds, and then he was just gone. A former teacher has since told Nancy that when she was working at the school, she would sometimes see a little boy standing on the front stairs.

There is a story of a little boy who drowned outside near the front steps in a ravine when there was a mudslide. Nancy has been unable to verify this story, and my research didn't turn up anything either.

The open door leads to the gym's bathroom, where Sam
captured an EVP of someone saying "Sammy."

Third Floor—Hallway/The Shadow

We were told that the third floor had been very active lately. In fact, a group that was there just the night before chased a shadow from the second floor up to the third floor. When they got to the third floor, the shadow just took off running down the hallway and was gone! The principal's office is up here. Who knows? Maybe the shadow was still running away from the principal? Nancy also showed us the original library, which was up here on the top floor until the librarian got bone cancer and lost a leg. The library was moved to the second floor after that. Library cards from the old card catalog system were still there, and I was very fascinated by that.

Sam and I set up in the hallway on the top floor just as the sun was going down. I was focusing on the window at the end of the hall when I saw something out of the corner of my eye. After you think you see something, it is very easy to dismiss it as a trick of the light or your mind and your vision playing tricks on you. But I went back and listened to what I said on the video recorder, and I'm convinced that I really did see a shadow person. At the moment it happened, I said to Sam, "I know what I saw. I saw a shadow come running out of that door and run back in. That's exactly what I saw. I blinked and it was gone." I then said out loud to whoever the shadow was, "I know I saw you. I know what I saw. Somebody saw you last night running around."

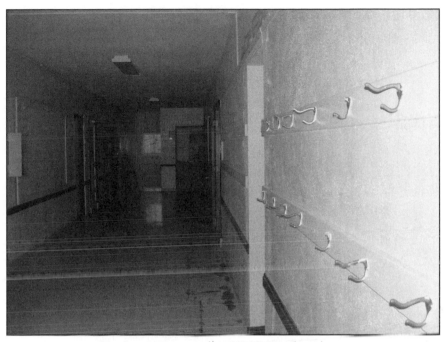

Shadow hallway on the third floor, where I saw
something pop out of a room and run back in.

Sam and I kept talking, trying to get something to interact with us using
the K2 or the flashlights, to no avail. I even promised I would share Sam's
stash of almond M&M's and said, "Well, maybe you don't know how to
turn that light on," hoping to entice him to prove me wrong. We couldn't get
anything to happen. Finally, we ended the session with me saying, "Maybe
you didn't mean for me to see you. I did though. I was seeing something
really weird. It was kid-size." I told Sam we needed to go set up in the room
on the right where I thought I saw the shadow dart out and see if we could
get something to happen. Boy, did we! I believe this transcript is significant
in backing up what I thought I saw out of the corner of my eye with the
shadow. See what you think from this excerpt:

Classroom on Top Floor, Across from the Auditorium

- ME: That K2 is doing something. It's going all the way to orange. If you're with us, can you turn one of those flashlights on?

  » Lights up.

- ME: Wow. Can you turn it back off for me? I've got the chills. I'm going to ask you some questions, and if your answer is yes, that's when you will turn the light on for me.

  » Lights up.

- ME: Okay, sounds good to me, too. Did I see you earlier? Did I see you step out of this room into that hallway?

  » Lights up. *(This blew my mind. It still does!)*

- ME: I thought so. Did you mean for me to see you?

  » Lights up. *(Blows MY MIND!)*

- ME: Just to confirm, did you mean for me to see you earlier when you stepped out into the hallway?

- ME: Did I see you?

- ME: Are you still here?

  » Lights up (twice in a row).

- ME: Did you go to school here? Remember, turning the light on means "yes."

  » Lights up.

- ME: Did you have class in this room?

  » Lights up.

- ME: Did you like school?

  » Lights up.

- ME: I liked school, too. I was really good at it. I pretty much spent as many years as I could doing it. Well...are you here by yourself?

  » Lights up.

- ME: Do you have friends here? Can you turn the light on if you've got friends here with you?

  » Lights up.

- ME: Well that's good. Are your friends in this room with us? Can you turn that light on if your friends are with us now?

  » Lights up.

- ME: Just two of you?

  » Lights up.

- ME: Are you a grown-up?

  » Lights up.

- ME: Did you teach school here?

  » Lights up.

- ME: Are you the librarian?

  » Lights up (two times—before I can even get the full question out!).

- ME: Do you live in Maxwell, Iowa? Are you from here?

  » Lights up.

- ME: Is it good to have someone to talk to?

  » Lights up.

• ME: Thank you. We like talking to you too. Can you say your name into the recorder? Tell us how long you've been here and what you're doing.

• ME: Do you ever go anywhere besides the school?
  » Lights up.

• ME: Well, I'm going to try and guess where else you go when you're not at this school house. One of the places I would guess is that maybe you go home?
  » Lights up.

• ME: Is your home close to the schoolhouse?

• ME: Does your family still live in your home?
  » Lights up.

• ME: You are giving me the chills. Does your family know that you go visit them? (Light flickers.) Do they know that you go back home? Do they ever get to talk to you? (K2 lights up).

• ME: Do you try to talk to them when you go back there?
  » Lights up.

• ME: I want to know, do you just go back home to kind of check in and make sure everybody is doing okay?

• ME: Just to look after them? Well, do you go home for a different reason than that? (K2 lights up to orange.)

• ME: So you go back home, and you come here, do you go anywhere else besides those two places?
  » Lights up.

FARRAR SCHOOL—MAXWELL, IOWA   115

• ME: Do you travel outside the city of Maxwell? (Light flickers.) Okay, just so I've got this right. To confirm. Does that mean that everywhere you go is somewhere in the city of Maxwell?

» Lights up.

• ME: Are you still here?

» Lights up.

• ME: Are you stuck here?

» Lights up.

• ME: Do you know why you're stuck here?

• ME: Do you know if you were in an accident?

» Lights up.

• ME: What happened to you? Can you tell us on the recorder what happened to you?

• ME: Did somebody hurt you?

» Lights up.

• ME: Do you know who it was?

• ME: Do you know how they hurt you?

• ME: Are you sure that somebody hurt you? Are you sure? It's okay.

» Lights up.

At this point, I start having the sense that she was some kind of murder victim or in a car accident.

- ME: Do you remember what happened? I don't want to upset you, and I don't want to talk about it if you don't want to talk about it, but if you do, then I want to know if you remember what happened.

  » Lights up.

- ME: Are you a female?

  » Lights up.

- ME: Did you get hurt by a man? Did a man hurt you?

- ME: Were you in a car accident?

- ME: Did you hurt yourself?

- ME: Do you not want to tell me?

  » Lights up.

- ME: That's okay. I'll quit asking you about it. It's okay if you don't want to talk about it.

- ME: Are you still here?

  » Lights up.

- SAM (to me): I guess they don't want to tell us.

- ME: I almost kind of think that you just came through because we were trying to talk to you. Is that what's going on? Are you here because of us?

  » Lights up.

- ME: Did we call you here? Wow. That's wild. You are giving me the chills.

- ME: I just have somebody telling me that they showed themselves to me on purpose, that I saw them, and that I called them here. Did I get that right? I saw you, you showed yourself to me on purpose, and you're here because we're trying to talk to somebody and you heard us so you came?
  » Lights up.

- ME: Is this the first time that we're talking—tonight?

- ME: I know you, don't I?
  » Lights up.

- ME: Why do I know you?

- ME: Do you go where I go?

- ME: Are you related to me?

- ME: Why do I know you?

- ME: Do you watch over me?
  » Lights up.

- ME (to Sam): Is this flipping you out?!?!? This is flipping me out!

This was so weird! Could we have been talking to the librarian? Was I talking to some sort of guardian angel or spirit who watches out for me? Was I talking to someone who had bad intentions and was going down this road with me to keep me interacting with them and engaged? We just don't know. To sum it up again: somebody was telling me that they showed themselves to me on purpose, that I saw them, and that I called them here. That is exactly what happened here. It blows my mind.

Third Floor—Auditorium

You will also find the auditorium on the top floor. You can tell right away that it was once a beautiful room, and to me, it still is. Nancy said they are in the process of fixing it up and returning it to its original glory days. These are your ghost hunting dollars at work, people! There has been a lot of activity reported in the auditorium. A woman was knocked flat on her back. Nancy said she went down like a tower that toppled over. Another woman was actually shoved to the ground. Many people have reported being touched by a phantom entity. We settled in on the stage in the auditorium. After just a few minutes, we captured the following EVP in there:

- ME: Has anybody been to Madison County and seen all of these covered bridges?
  » UNKNOWN MALE: **Yes.**

Second Floor

On the second floor, Nancy had a personal experience when she was with her sister and her friend Jackie. Jackie is a psychic, and she said, "There is a little girl here who needs to move on." After Jackie spoke, Nancy saw a light come toward her and then go right through her. She felt a huge knot in her stomach and chest. She said her stomach hurt for three days after that experience. Her sister then saw an apparition of a little girl go by.

A classroom on the second floor, which was
the site of my last session for the evening.

I was completely drained from the hour-long flashlight session we just had, plus I was recovering from a migraine earlier in the day. By this point, I was begging off so I could go sleep on the sofa in Nancy's safe room. Sam walked me back to the safe room and took off alone for a solo investigation.

The Farrar school exceeded our expectations by far, and we had a great investigation! Also, we love Iowa!

From the playground equipment in the front of the schoolyard, you can have a nice view of the graveyard. A beautiful yet chilling scene.

Outside the schoolhouse as a storm was brewing.

If You Decide to Visit:

Location & Contact Info

11125 NE 134th Avenue

Maxwell, IA 50161

Tel: 515-577-4213

Email: *ftvnancy@hotmail.com*

Owner: Nancy and James Oliver

Website

www.hauntingatfarrar.com

Type of Tours/Hunts Offered

Private; Hosts public events throughout the year

Haunted attraction for Halloween? Yes

Bathroom facilities? Yes—bathrooms are downstairs in the gym.

Safe room for sleeping/snacking? Yes—and they get our best safe room award!

Size: 17,000 sq. ft.

Price: Friday and Saturday night rates are $240 for up to six people ($40 for each additional guest); Sunday–Thursday night rates are $180 for up to six people ($30 for each additional guest).

Tips: No need to book a hotel in connection with your investigation. Two people can sleep in the safe room on the couches perfectly fine!

Closest airports: Des Moines International Airport—28 miles away; Kansas City International Airport—192 miles away.

Media Appearances

My Ghost Story, Season 2—5/21/11

My Ghost Story, Season 4—4/28/12

Sam's Observations

Going Solo at Farrar

When Jamie first mentioned the Farrar School to me, I asked her, "Why is an old schoolhouse supposedly haunted?" After visiting there, I believe that there still is no clear-cut answer. During our tour of the building, Nancy showed us the "safe room." In it was a coffee maker, couches, mini-fridge, even a television! When Jamie and I saw this room, we both looked at each other and said, "Jackpot!" We had already decided that we were going to try and sleep for a couple of hours in our rental car before our 6:30 a.m. flight back to Atlanta. With two comfortable couches available, there was no need to do that!

Now, there comes a time in every investigation when Jamie is just done. You can just see it in her face. That girl needs her rest! So when it came time for her to call it a night, I walked her back to the safe room and decided that I wanted to walk the building by myself. I wanted to go back to the areas that we had investigated previously to see if I could pick up any more evidence. I wanted to see if anything would be different, since I would be alone. I took a flashlight, the IR camera, the K2, and the digital recorder.

I walked the building from top floor to bottom floor and didn't experience anything. I stopped a few minutes at each location. I ended up in the gymnasium and decided to use the restroom before heading back up to the safe room. I turned off all of the equipment (or so I thought) and sat everything on a table that was right inside the restroom door.

When I started to gather everything to leave, I noticed that I forgot to turn off the digital recorder. I am not sure if I consider this a good thing or a bad thing.

When I got home and started going through the evidence, I was shocked at what I heard after putting the equipment down on that table. You can clearly hear someone say "Sammy," then some indiscernible whispering.

It's a fairly good-size restroom, as you might expect, being next to a school's gymnasium. Even so, I know that I was alone in there. Jamie was asleep upstairs, and the Olivers hadn't left their living area all night.

What's really strange about this is that I was called "Sammy." Jamie only calls me "Sam," and I was introduced only as "Sam" to Nancy earlier that evening. I believe that whatever was trying to get my attention knew me from somewhere else. I grew up being called "Sammy" and still have some family and close friends that call me by that name.

Back at St. Albans Sanatorium in Radford, Virginia, we were told a theory by a member of the Mountain Ridge Paranormal Research Society. These "haunted" locations may be a beacon to unrested spirits. If you were one of these spirits, wouldn't you want to go where people are continually trying to communicate with you? This seems reasonable to me.

I could not believe it when I first heard my name being called on that recording! It was mind-blowing. I've never had anything like this happen to me at any other location. This was so personal. It kind of lends credence to the "haunted" locations being beacons because no one knows me as "Sammy" in the state of Iowa.

SEVEN

Tooele Hospital/
Asylum 49—
Tooele, Utah

The old Tooele Hospital was built in 1949 and shut down in 2002. Before the hospital was built, the land housed the county poor farm.

While in operation, nurses recount stories of hearing moans and cries from the empty delivery room. It happened so frequently that the nurses bought a television and placed it near the delivery room door to drown out the phantom moans!

It is said that a spiritual portal exists here and that it is guarded by a nurse named Maria.

On page 75 of *Talking to Yourself in the Dark*, Tom Carr describes his investigation at the hospital and a disturbing EVP: "Kill your patient." He has seen a nurse in the maternity ward caring for patients who are no longer there and believes that the spirit of a little girl has followed him home.

Tooele Hospital/Asylum 49.

Our Experiences—June 16, 2012, Private Investigation

The location of the hospital is rather peculiar—on its right side is a sprawling cemetery. We were met by one of the owners, Dusty, and she was kind enough to show us around the hospital and tell us some of the history and paranormal stories. People frequently make obnoxious wisecracks about the hospital being a "ghost factory" because of its proximity to the cemetery. Dusty assured me, they weren't thinking anything like that when they purchased the building in 2006. The purpose was to build a Halloween haunted attraction. They had no idea what they were getting into at the time.

Dusty does not believe that anyone is trapped there. If they come across someone who seems to be trapped, she said they get every religious head they can find to move them on. She said she wants spirits to come and go as they please and not have a location that is a sort of spiritual jail. They seem to have a lot of travelers here.

Sometimes people have had experiences where the ghosts think they are doing something funny (to them—it's not funny to anyone else!) and then have later been captured on someone's voice recorder saying they're sorry. A lot of the reported phenomena is thought to be residual energy—for instance, babies crying or crawling on the floor over in the maternity wing. But there have been plenty of intelligent interactions reported as well.

One such intelligent spirit is a little girl who frequently frightens the staff working the haunted attraction by darting in and out from underneath hospital beds!

Shadow people have been reported to walk the hallways. Most recently, a shadow-type entity has made itself known by bouncing around the walls in the maternity wing. A former patient by the name of Wesley likes the room on the right at the end of the hall. Doors have shut on command. The spirit of a woman shows up from time to time to visit her babies.

The maternity-wing hallway, where several entities have reportedly been seen, including something that bounces from floor to ceiling.

The room at the end of the labor and delivery hall on the left felt a little "off" to me. I spoke up and said something to Dusty, and she said that several people have had that same reaction in that room. I walked out of it and didn't return the rest of the day or night.

One thing they have here that I have never seen anywhere else before—a mirror gazing room. They have a room set up with a chair facing a mirror. The mirror is raised slightly above where your reflection would be, so what you are seeing in the mirror is something else other than your own reflection. One psychic has said that there are always two angels in this room. Sam and I did not try this out. Quite frankly, I was too scared.

The conference room in the middle of the hospital seems to be a hotspot for interacting with child spirits. You will know you are in the right place when you see the toys that other investigators have brought into the building.

The ER side had a slightly creepier vibe—even in the daytime. Dusty told us that they were doing an extreme ghost hunting reenactment of a patient who died of a bullet wound, and people were having their K2s and flashlights lighting up like crazy. They also captured an EVP that said: "Caught a bullet." (Note: We listened to it, and it is a Class A find!)

Another spirit that has been known to show up on the ER side is known as The Guardian. They are not sure what he is up to, but he is an ominous shadow figure.

Another paranormal experiment that we learned about is called "The Human Pendulum." There is a room in the ER where if you hold your arms out and ask the spirits to show you what "yes" is, they will push you forward or backward. The opposite direction means "no." And you can communicate that way. I do not like to invite anything to touch me, so I didn't try it out.

Dusty was the first person who mentioned the idea to me that spirits may be able to move between earth and heaven. I thought that was a fascinating theory, and certainly one that I hadn't even considered before!

Dusty was kind enough to bring her computer out and share some of the evidence that has been collected over the years. They have, by far, the single best photo I have seen to date—a little girl apparition (thought to be named Emily) outside the nursery, peering in from the hallway. The moment I saw that photo, I was covered in chills head to toe. The photo reminded me of a recent horror movie that involved a little girl with long, dark hair, a videotape, and a well.

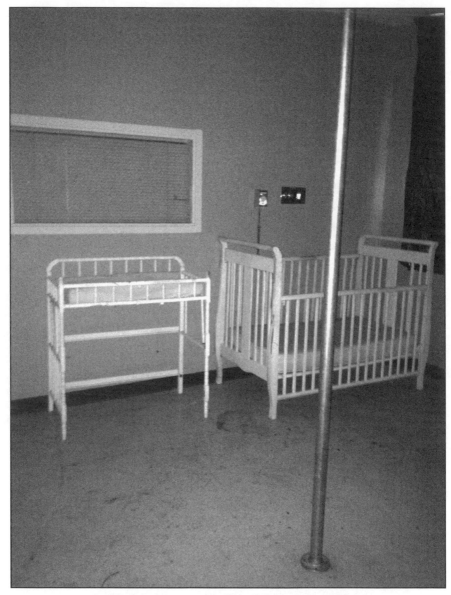

Inside the nursery, where I had the most touching,
weird, life-changing experience to date.

We had a life-changing experience in that nursery. Here is an excerpt from the transcript. See what you think about what happened to us.

Nursery—Angel Hospital?

- ME (to Sam): Did you just see something? *Someone's trying to make that light in the far right go off,* I thought.

- ME: If that's you—try it a little bit more. I don't know, I was looking somewhere else, but I saw something flicker down there.

- SAM: I've just got a camera in my hand. Don't be afraid of it either. I'm sure you've seen people walking around with cameras. We're not here to try and hurt you or anything like that. We're just trying to talk to you. We'd like you to try and talk to us.
  » Lights up—flashlight on far right (just like I was seeing earlier).

- ME: Are you still here?

- ME (to Sam): What are you looking at?

- SAM: Just looking around.

- ME: That creeps me out.

- ME: I think something is wrong with that flashlight.

- SAM: Jamie doesn't believe that anyone is here, but if someone is here with us, can you turn that flashlight on again just to show her that it's not just a malfunctioning flashlight?

- ME: Kind of seemed like it was.

• ME: You can jump in with it at any time.

» Lights up.

• ME: Do you know Dusty?

• SAM: I think she said she's pretty much up here every day.

• ME: How about Kim? Do you know who Kim is?

» Light flickers.

• ME: Was that a yes for Kim? You know who Kim is?

» Lights up.

• ME: Am I running through my questions too fast?

» Lights up.

• ME: Okay, I'm sorry. I'll slow it down. I'm sorry. It's just weird. I mean, you obviously can hear us, but we can't hear you. I mean, it just sucks. It's the craziest thing. Can you see us?

» Lights up.

• ME: Are you sitting in that rocking chair across from me?

• ME: Are you here with one other friend?

» Lights up.

• ME: Cool. Do any of you talk to people who come in here a lot?

• ME: All right, well I've got a new question for you. It's kind of serious. My boss wanted me to ask you. Is there a heaven?

» Lights up.

• ME: Uh, that's a positive. There's a heaven.

- SAM: I know that.

- ME: Okay, have you seen it?
  » Lights up.

- ME: Do you go ... I don't even know how to ask this, but,
  are you in your heaven? I mean, we're on earth, but are you
  like on another plane? Are you in heaven right now, talking
  to us from heaven?
  » Lights up.

- ME (to Sam): Holy crap. Is that possible?

- SAM: I don't know.

- ME: Is there a specific reason why you're trying to talk
  to us right now?

- ME: Are you ever lonely?
  » Lights up.

- ME: I'm sorry.

- ME: Can you tell me if you died here in this hospital?
  » Lights up. (K2 going off to the midway point.)

- ME: I want to know more about what heaven is. Did you
  believe in God before you died? Were you a Christian?
  » Lights up.

- SAM: I keep seeing things moving around. It felt like
  something touched my leg and then my hip.

- ME: Did somebody just touch Sam? Can you light
  that light up?

- ME: Is Sam just imagining stuff? Let us know if Sam is just imagining stuff.
  » Lights up.

- ME: I think that there's six people in here. Am I right?
  » Lights up.

- ME: We heard two different stories about angels tonight. And I didn't believe it.
  » Lights up.

- ME: But I think I do now. Were they true? These stories?
  » Lights up.

- ME: What are a couple of angels doing in this place? I mean, is that what it is—have you been following me around?
  » Lights up.

- ME: Just here in this hospital you've been following me around? Everywhere?
  » Lights up.

- ME: For always?
  » Lights up.

- ME: Have I ever seen you?

- ME: How I feel right now is that there is such a good presence here with me right now that I feel like I could walk around the whole hospital and be okay. In the total darkness, without my flashlight. And I would be okay. (K2 goes to orange.)

- SAM: I see a bunch of stuff moving around to the left of me.

• ME: Kim used the phrase "guardian angel." (K2 lights up again.) Is Kim right?

» Lights up.

• ME: I'm telling you. We're in the presence of something. This is something different.

CONVERSATION BETWEEN ME AND SAM:

• ME: Am I crazy? I really feel like I'm talking to an angel. (K2 lights up, light comes on again.)

• SAM: It could possibly well be.

• ME: Is that possible?

• SAM: Sure it's possible. Angels are real.

• ME: It's very odd. (K2 lights up, light comes on again).

• ME: It told me I needed to stop doing this because I already found what I was looking for.

• SAM: I promise you, when I was standing over there against the wall, looking out into the hallway, I saw a bunch of … somethings … coming in here.

• ME: I almost feel like he's telling me not to tempt fate, almost. You know what I mean? Like, don't go around in the dark looking for something because you may not like what you find.

• SAM: I don't think that's the case. I just don't feel that.

• ME: I just had the weirdest experience.

- SAM: I think it was a good experience.

- ME: I mean, it was real to me.

- SAM: Yeah, me too.

- ME: I'm tired. That thing told me to stop.

- SAM: No, that's not what it said. Do you want to go somewhere else?

- ME: I want to go home.

After this session, I was serious about wanting to go home. If there was a flight back to Atlanta that night, I would have been on it. This was the strangest and most transformative experience in my life. I wanted to get out of there and kind of just let it all soak in. I still find it mind-boggling. I included the transcript here, even though it is highly personal. I will not share the video with the world, because for some reason, Sam is panning the camera all over the room (he said he kept seeing shadows out of the corner of his eye and was trying to capture them) instead of just fixating on the flashlights. Also, for some reason he videos me crying. Obviously I don't want to share such a raw moment with strangers.

That was the only time in my life where I felt just absolutely shrouded in what I can only describe as a feeling of sheer joy. I felt surrounded by pure goodness. It wiped away any possible doubts that I may have had about the existence of angels and heaven. It was truly an amazing experience, and I think for whatever reason, I needed it to happen to me at that particular time. The experience will never leave me.

Both Sam and I regret not staying longer for our private investigation. But I was worn out and overwhelmed by my experience, and I had to get out of there.

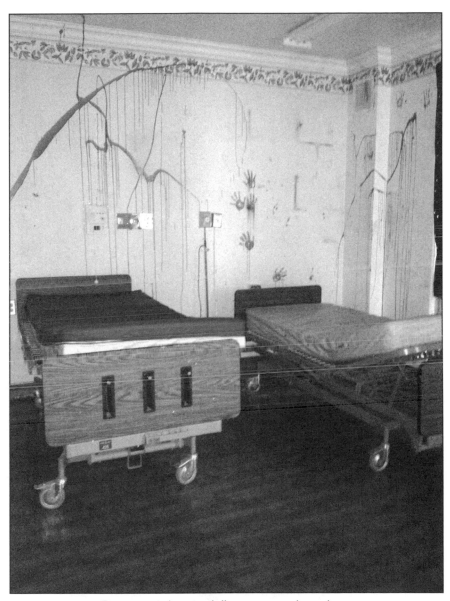

Room next door to delivery room, where doors
have opened and shut on their own.

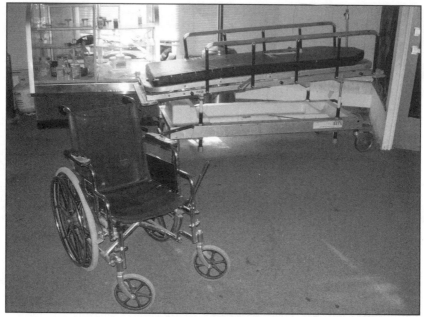

All of the equipment/furniture throughout the hospital was inherited
with the building when the owners purchased it in 2006.

If You Decide to Visit:

Location & Contact Info

140 E. 200 S.

Tooele, UT 84074

Contact: Dusty Kingston, owner

Email: *dusty@asylum49.com*

Website

www.asylum49.com

Type of Tours/Hunts Offered

Various private packages offered—see website.

Haunted attraction for Halloween? Yes

Bathroom facilities? Yes

Safe room for sleeping/snacking? Yes

Price: $240 for up to eight people and $30 per person after that.

Tips: Spend some time in nearby Park City. Don't miss Ruth's Diner in Salt Lake City.

Closest airport: Salt Lake City International Airport—24 miles away.

Media Appearances

Ghost Adventures, Season 4, Episode 26—5/27/11

- *The World's Fastest Indian*

- *The Stand*

Sam's Observations

Tooele Hospital was a different investigation compared to the other locations that we've visited.

While we were in the nursery doing a flashlight/EVP session, Jamie's line of questioning and the responses that we were getting led us to believe that we may have been communicating with an angel.

During this session, I noticed a lot of shadowy movement right outside the room. This movement seemed to hover around the periphery of the room but did not enter.

I believe in angels. I believe that they have saved my bacon on more than one occasion. Angels have long been associated with mercy and hospitals. Who knows if we were speaking with an angel? I'd like to believe that we were. I do know that Jamie had a deep and moving experience inside Old Tooele Hospital.

EIGHT

MANSFIELD REFORMATORY — MANSFIELD, OHIO

Construction began on the Ohio State Reformatory in 1886, but because of construction delays, the first groups of inmates weren't able to be transferred from the Ohio Penitentiary until 1896. Sherri Brake discusses the purpose of creating a reformatory on page 47 of *The Haunted History of the Ohio State Reformatory*:

> *The whole idea of a reformatory was new in this time frame. It was being built with the progressive philosophy of the late nineteenth century, when it was hoped that reforming young men would be*

accomplished by segregating them from hardened criminals. The reformatory was to motivate the occupants to live fuller lives and motivate them to be better people as a whole.

An admirable goal, but certainly one that was much harder to live up to than anyone had anticipated. The reformatory was criticized as early as 1933 as being overcrowded. By 1978, a council was formed on behalf of the inmates by various churches and civic groups, and a lawsuit was filed citing constitutional rights violations. The reformatory was housing 2,200 inmates in a building designed to hold a maximum of 1,200 people, and inmates were exposed to inhumane conditions. The lawsuit was actually resolved in 1983, and the prison was ordered to close by 1986. Delays were in full swing, but the prison was finally closed down in 1990.

Mansfield Reformatory.

Our Experiences—
July 14, 2012 Day Tour and Public Investigation

My first thought was, it looks like a castle, not a prison. Hence the nickname that I later read about: "Dracula's Castle." The administration buildings are beautiful, and you can tell that the Preservation Society has worked hard to restore and maintain them. You can easily spend hours wandering around the place during the day, and we did just that on a self-guided tour. This location has a lot of appeal for tourists in general because of the connection to the movie *The Shawshank Redemption.*

Some areas were closed off to us on the day tour, including the sub-basement, the upper floor of solitary, and many of the catwalks in the cell blocks. During the ghost hunt, though, we had access to about 98 percent of the building. We didn't come across any area that we wanted to go in that was blocked off. This was amazing!

One of the rooms that I had a sense about during our daytime tour was up in dignitary housing on the third floor of the warden's quarters. You'll know you're in the right place because of the blue walls and the stage in the area used to entertain guests. Later that night, our guide told us a story about this very room. And I thought to myself again, yep, nailed that one too. There is a chair in the middle of the room that a spirit is very particular about. He doesn't mind a bit if a female sits in the chair but will get upset if a male takes his seat as his own. Our guide told us that one guy asked, "What are you going to do to me?" The response on the voice recorder simply said, "Stairway." I bet that guy was extremely careful when he went back downstairs!

Up in the old warden's quarters, Helen may make her presence known with the scent of her perfume. If you experience this, let one of the guides know what you smell so they can corroborate your experience.

Before we entered the building for the ghost hunt, Scott told us about talking to other owners of famous haunted locations and their calling around and asking each other if they've noticed an increase in activity by new people (ghost travelers) this year—as if something is stirring things up and spirits are moving around. Very interesting!

We went on about a ninety-minute tour with our guide before we were turned loose and before they turned the lights off. We started up in the Catholic chapel. We were told that at one time, people from town would attend church here right along with the prisoners. Recent activity includes a lot of EVPs.

This hallway on the second floor of the administration building and the stairwell leading to the chapel had a lot of traffic. However, it was mostly used by citizen churchgoers and workers, not prisoners.

The reformatory chapel drew parishoners from town who came to hear the exact same sermon as the prisoners. The prisoners sat on the main floor as pictured, and citizens of Mansfield sat on a higher level.

The room above the chapel is the original hospital, which later became the TB ward. Sam and I knew this and had already been up there during the day tour and noted that we needed to return for the night investigation. Our guide told us that just last night a shadow was seen three different times at the back of this room. (This is exactly where we had our experience right after the tour!)

TB Ward—Floor above Chapel

This was our very first stop for the evening. It was HOT up here! Our guide told everyone to wait until the night cooled off the area before heading upstairs, so we went early to have a better chance of some uninterrupted time. We figured correctly in that regard. Within a few minutes, we were settled in and focused on the end of the room (our backs were to the entrance). Moonlight was pouring in from the windows, so we weren't in complete darkness. We could see the lights from the new prison that borders the property here as well. Suddenly, I thought I saw something dart out of the last room on the left. I said to Sam, "I know what I saw. I saw movement." Sam replied, "I saw it too." This wasn't a typical black shadow person. This was more of a lighter shadow or gray mist that moved. We walked down to that last room on the left and found out that it was a closet! So what we were seeing was not someone's car lights driving by. Could it have been some sort of trick of the eye? Some light phenomenon? I guess. But what kind of light trick makes you think you see something run out of a closet? Certainly not a trick that I ever experienced before or since!

We were advised against provoking and were told it is best to keep things on an even keel. "Keep in mind where you are. You're in prison," our guide said. But on the other hand, don't confine your ghost hunting just to prison. Before Mansfield was built, the land was used as a training ground for soldiers in the Civil War. And even before that, it was an Indian settlement. One guide has reported to be in weekly communication with a Civil War soldier. Another tip we received was that it is easier to watch shadows move along the west block catwalk since there are fewer bars on the tiers.

Solitary

Solitary is considered one of the prison's most active areas. Our guide shared a personal experience with us. He said he has actually seen a bust of a male apparition in a cell in the solitary section.

There is also an infamous story of two inmates being forced to share a cell in solitary—with only one emerging alive. The missing inmate was found stuffed under a bunk.

Visitor's Room Upstairs in Solitary

This was one of those great areas that was off-limits during our day tour. As soon as I saw the area, I immediately thought it would be a great place to try to do a flashlight session. We set up our things and got situated on the side where the visitors would have been. And we prepared ourselves to have a visit. I was not wrong about this spot! Sam set the flashlights down on the counter on the right side of the room and immediately one lit up. I went through a series of questions but could not get anything to happen—the light just remained on. I declared that the light was loose, and Sam announced that he was going to walk over there and turn that light off manually. He did, and I began the session again. I was probably about seven or eight minutes in, just talking to myself in the dark, when I thought I saw the same sort of gray mist materialize like the one above the chapel earlier that evening. I don't even know if "mist" is the right way to describe it—it just was some substance that made the darkness a little lighter. Sort of like a shadow person, but made up of a lighter color, and not in the shape of an actual person. I continued talking because I knew I was right, that this was going to be an opportunity to capture some more evidence, and I remained fully convinced that what I was feeling was real. The last thing I said before the light finally turned on again was, "Can you please just turn it on so I know that I'm not crazy?!?" The flashlight lit right up and we were back on again. Here is an excerpt from our session:

- ME: That's really cool. Can you let us know if you were a prisoner here?
  » Lights up.

- ME: This might be silly, and I apologize if it is, if I'm insulting your intelligence in any way, but one of the things we don't know when we're trying to talk to you is if we're both thinking that it's the same time period. Today's date is July 14, 2012. Did you know that?

- ME: Did you think it was a different day?
  » Lights up.

- ME: Are you stuck here?
  » Lights up.

- ME: I'm sorry, that must be horrible.

- ME: Are there other people here with you who are stuck? too?
  » Lights up.

- ME: Okay. Turn it back off for me.

- ME (to Sam): What the crap is that? It sounds like someone is walking towards me. It freaked me out.

- ME: Was that you making that noise?

- ME: Was that one of your friends making noise?

- ME: Are you still here with me?
  » Lights up.

- ME: Okay. I'm trying to talk, and to figure stuff out. Bear with me. I know it has got to be a frustrating process. I hope you said your name in that recorder. (**EVP RESPONSE: Eugene Carter**). Do you mind confirming for us just one more time that you were a prisoner here? Can you turn that light back on?

- SAM: One thing I would like to know. You may be talking to us and we can't hear you. Jamie tried to confirm that you were a prisoner here, and nothing was happening.
  » Lights up.

- SAM: One thing that would be really neat to know— why were you in here? If you could just tell us out loud.

- SAM: Do you like (lights up) to have people in here like us trying to talk to you?
  » **EVP RESPONSE: F*** you.**

- ME: Do you talk to people a lot? (You can hear some people shuffle by the room making noise. Sam tells him not to get scared off.)

- SAM: Are you still here with us?
  » Lights up.

- ME: I bet you hated having to take a shower here.
  » Lights up.

- ME: Let it go for me. Thank you. Can you tell me, first of all, were you guilty of what they said you did? It's okay to admit it, I'm not going to quit talking to you if you were. I just want to know, honestly. Did you do what they said that you did?

- ME: Are you telling me that you're innocent?
  » Lights up.

- ME: And you know, there's the old joke about—nobody in prison is guilty. You know what I'm talking about? Are you really telling me that you're innocent? If that's what you're telling me, then I'll believe you. I will. Were you just joking with me?

- ME: Light that light up one more time if you're telling me that you were innocent.
  » Lights up.

- ME: Oh my God. Okay, I believe you. Please tell me your name.

- ME: Does your family believe that you're innocent?

- ME: Did anybody? Did anybody believe you?
  » Lights up.

• ME: It upsets me that you were innocent and that you're stuck here now.

This session was absolutely heartbreaking to me. Whoever we were talking to, I felt that he was innocent. I could feel it. To watch him indicate with the light that he was stuck there—and that others were stuck there—was just so sad and so terrible to me. And there was absolutely nothing that I could do about it but walk away and leave him there.

To not find peace in death—to be stuck somewhere—maybe that is exactly what hell is. It sure sounds like it to me. That terrifies me. I don't want to get trapped somewhere in death. I don't seriously think that is a possibility for me, but the thought is terrifying.

A popular theory that I've heard several times about prisoners is that they believed that if they died in prison, their souls would be trapped there. You have to wonder—if that is what they truly believe in, is this a self-fulfilling prophecy? For instance, if you believe you will be trapped, then you are. Likewise, if you believe in God and heaven, then that's what happens to you. If you believe you are free to roam around wherever you want, then you'd be free to do so.

I am becoming more inclined or persuaded to think that if you have found peace in life and developed a solid belief system, then that is what you are going to get in death. Quite simply, if you are a lost soul in life, you're going to be a lost soul in death, too.

Note: When Sam played the EVP of what sounds like the guy saying his name—Eugene Carter—I had chills all over. I immediately emailed the clip to the Preservation Society to find out if they had any record of this inmate. I also ran his name through the online database of Ohio's Department of Corrections but did not get any hits. We don't know who he is.

Visiting in solitary. I just had a feeling about this place. We captured a great flashlight session along with an EVP of someone responding "Eugene Carter" when we asked for a name.

Sub-Basement

A female guide had a bad experience in the sub-basement, where she felt as though someone was invading her space, and now she refuses to go back down there. Later, I attempted to explore this area but was smacked hard in the face with such a bad smell (dead animal maybe?) that I couldn't stay down there for more than a few seconds after going down the short staircase.

Two guards were killed by prisoners while they were on duty, Urban Wilford in 1926 and then Frank Hanger in 1932. Urban was seventy-two and was shot outside the west gate during an unsuccessful escape attempt. Frank was beaten with an iron bar during an escape attempt. However, it was much more common for inmates to violently attack one another. There have been two hundred known murders reported.

West cell block, the newest section of the prison.

A random 7' x 9' cell I picked to do a session in. Cozy digs.

Rows and rows of cells on the East cell block. A truly humbling site.

I did not think anything was going on in this cell when I was in there. Sam stood outside the cell on the catwalk. I just sat there and felt the claustrophobia and the sadness. It is no stretch of the imagination to feel the walls closing in and pressing down on you. You become an animal in a cage within seconds. We got home and found out we captured a Class A EVP of someone answering my question!

- ME: Do you just want to talk to me, by myself?
» RESPONSE: **Yes.**

Wow!

All in all, this was a very nicely run public hunt. The place is big enough to do it. We had a few stressful moments with people walking in on us or passing by, but nothing that ruined the night or got us too stressed out. And the human traffic certainly didn't seem to interfere with the activity we experienced! Upon leaving, Sam asked me if I thought I could ever do an investigation in there, just the two of us. I said I thought I could. He looked at me as though he didn't believe me. Not one bit.

If You Decide to Visit:

Location & Contact Info:

100 Reformatory Road
Mansfield, OH 44905
Tel: 419-522-2644
Fax: 419-522-8492
Email: *contact@mrps.org*

Website

www.mrps.org

Type of Tours/Hunts Offered

Various historic tours offered; Public and private ghost events.

Haunted attraction for Halloween? Yes

Bathroom facilities? Yes, and they were very clean too!

Safe room for sleeping/snacking? Not for sleeping, but for snacking and taking breaks.

Size: Around 250,000 sq. ft.

Price: $70 per person for public hunt. Private events on Friday and Saturday night for up to thirty people is $2,400; Sunday–Thursday night rate for private events up to 15 people = $1,200.

Tips: Don't worry about packing late night snacks of your own. Mansfield was the only place that kept us both fed and hydrated. Pizza and drinks = VERY nice touch by Mansfield!

Closest airports: Port Columbus International Airport—56 miles away; Cleveland Hopkins International Airport—57 miles away; Akron-Canton Regional Airport—57 miles away; Detroit Metropolitan Wayne County Airport—109 miles away; Pittsburgh International Airport—121 miles away.

Media Appearances

Ghost Hunters, Season 2, Episode 212—10/12/05

The Most Terrifying Places in America—2008

Ghost Adventures, Season 3, Episode 5—11/20/09

Ghost Hunters Academy—6/30/10

Paranormal Challenge—7/8/11

Fox Family's *Scariest Places on Earth*

Real Scary Stories

- *The Shawshank Redemption*

- *Air Force One*

- *Tango & Cash*

Sam's Observations

What an amazing experience—investigating at Mansfield Reformatory! Not only is it said to be notoriously haunted, it was also used as the setting of one of my favorite movies, *The Shawshank Redemption*. Exploring the building and grounds and seeing where parts of the movie were shot (while on the daytime tour) was just as much fun as investigating the place for paranormal activity at night.

As far as the investigation goes, Jamie's intuition was right on the money in picking out the Visitation Room to investigate. We had a great flashlight/EVP session there. If who we were communicating with was being honest, then he was wrongfully sentenced to Mansfield. But to paraphrase a quote in *Shawshank*: "Everyone in prison is innocent."

We did get some good evidence. I was even cussed out by a male EVP! He thought we were laughing at him, but Jamie and I were laughing at the excitement from the flashlight lighting up. What a surreal experience to be cussed at by a ghost.

NINE

WEST VIRGINIA
PENITENTIARY—
MOUNDSVILLE,
WEST VIRGINIA

"Blood Alley." "Hell on Earth." These were the nicknames given to West Virginia Penitentiary. The Department of Justice called it one of the bloodiest institutions in the United States. The prison was established in July of 1866 and opened in 1867. It was designed to accommodate 840 men and 32 women. (The women were moved to another facility in 1947.) By the 1930s, it was extremely overcrowded, housing more than

2,700 inmates. This meant that up to three inmates were squeezed into a five-by-seven-foot cell.

In Sherri Brake's *The Haunted History of the West Virginia Penitentiary*, she discusses Warden Adams and the great changes he was trying to make to the prison in 1958. He asked the Federal Bureau of Prisons for help, and a representative went out and toured West Virginia Penitentiary. The representative told the warden: "I only know of one thing that ought to be done. You ought to call in the Air Force and bomb the place off the face of the earth."

West Virginia Penitentiary.

Methods of Torture Used in the Early Days

• Whippings with a cat-o'-nine-tails

• Kicking Jenny

• Shoo-Fly

The Kicking Jenny was a device invented at the prison. The inmate was stripped naked and bent over the machine in such a way that his legs were still standing up, but his chest was laid across the apparatus. Both legs and hands were secured with ropes. The prisoner was then beaten with a leather whip until he was almost dead.

The Shoo-Fly was when someone was placed in the stocks and blasted in the face with ice-cold water from a hose until the inmate was partly strangled to death.

Two Major Violent Prison Riots—1973 and 1986

The riot in 1973 was reported to have started when an inmate committed arson and injured some guards and two other inmates. Five guards were actually held hostage for twenty-four hours. The prisoners submitted a list of fifteen demands, twelve of which Governor Arch A. Moore, Jr. granted. One of the demands included removing ten solitary confinement cells in the basement. One inmate was killed during this riot.

In *West Virginia Penitentiary*, Jonathan D. Clemins states that on New Year's Day 1986, about sixteen officers called in sick, leaving only thirty-one to work the entire prison. According to procedure, the prisons should have been on lockdown because of the low number of employees, but it wasn't. As a result, during dinner, twenty inmates armed themselves with knives and stormed the mess hall. Three inmates who were thought to be snitches were killed during the forty-two-hour riot. This time, the demands were related to poor living conditions, such as the infestation of rats and cockroaches, spoiled maggot-infested food, sewage problems, and poor medical care.

Closure of the Prison

Finally, in 1989, the prison conditions were deemed to constitute cruel and unusual punishment, and West Virginia Penitentiary was closed for good in 1995.

The total death toll is documented at 998; however, it is thought to be much higher. Only 104 were actually executed by the state of West Virginia. The remaining deaths were murders or suicides.

Our Experiences—
July 21, 2012: Day Tour and Public Investigation

We arrived early enough in the afternoon to take the day tour of the prison. The tour did not take us into the administration building, which was extremely disappointing to us, since this is the beautiful castle-type structure. We were told, however, that there are plans to renovate this section of the building and turn it into a B&B, which we look forward to seeing. The day tour also skipped the psych hospital, the "Sugar Shack," and the basement. One fun thing that they did do was put us on lockdown in New Wall, a recently added section of the prison. Sam did it, not me. I wasn't taking any chances in there! I watched the guard flip a switch and stood back against the wall as the doors secured the volunteer inmates in their cells.

A family on the tour with us actually captured a shadow figure on video in the cafeteria right in the middle of the afternoon! My impression even during the day was how depressing this place is and must have been for the prisoners. The walls still have a distinct salty smell of sweat and just old mustiness. It's gross. I don't know how else to describe it. Sam didn't notice it, so maybe it was just me being an empath again. We had the benefit of having a former guard as a tour guide. One of the things we asked him was if there was any paranormal activity going on while the prison was still open. "Oh yes," he said. Guards would frequently report seeing someone walking in the yard only to have someone go out there and check on it and find no one.

New Wall, the most recently added cell block
at the prison, where Sam did his lockdown time.

The tour prior to the ghost hunt took us everywhere! While we were in the kitchen, our K2 lit all the way up to red several times! We were told that a lot of great evidence had been captured in there. We knew that to be true because of the family's video that we saw earlier in the day, plus we knew about Polly Gear's famous photo of the shadow man that had been captured standing by the door leading to the cafeteria. (A print of the photo is on display in the gift shop. Also, see Sherri Brake's *The Haunted History of the West Virginia Penitentiary* for a detailed description by Polly herself and the experiments attempted to debunk the photo.)

The North Hall, called the most dangerous housing unit in the United States in the 1990s, is where prisoners were locked down twenty-three hours a day. This was a prison within the prison. People were never sent directly here—they were always sent here as punishment for acts perpetrated while in the prison. One of the most haunting images that still comes to mind is the lone gun cage where one guard would sit and point his weapon at the cell block—ready to shoot at any given moment. That is one disturbing building over there.

Only the ground floor of North Hall was open for us (both during the day tour and the ghost hunt). We were shown the old cell that housed Red Snyder, an inmate who was brutally stabbed by another inmate in 1996 while in his cell. One former guard, Maggie, was on one paranormal show recounting a story of Red Snyder still greeting her when she walks by.

We got to see the R. D. Wall basement room and the Sugar Shack on our tour. R. D. Wall was tortured and murdered in the basement in 1979 for being a perceived snitch. The Sugar Shack was an indoor recreation room where inmates were unsupervised. As you might imagine, it was a virtual free-for-all down there. The nickname came from all of the sexual assaults and other sexual activity that went on down there. I told Sam to get it all stored in his mind because I wasn't going back down there later in the night by ourselves. Because of the bats, of course.

The solitary cell where the knocking originated.

Psych Ward—Solitary Confinement Cell Room

This was one of those places. I just knew as soon as I walked into the room. I told Sam we needed to get back up here first thing after our tour was over. We hoofed it right back over here immediately, and stuff started happening to us within just a few minutes. Our guide told us that he has heard knocking coming from inside this solitary cell:

Excerpt from full video:

- ME: Well did you just come here because we called you? Because we wanted to talk to somebody tonight? Is that why you came?

  » Lights up.

- ME: Did you see us on our tour earlier? Do you remember us from earlier today?

  » Lights up.

- ME: So does that mean that you just saw us when we came through here at nighttime with our bigger group? Maybe I've got it wrong.

  » Lights up.

- ME: Can you tell me—are you stuck here? That's one of the things that I always want to know. It's really important to me.

- ME: So does that mean you can go wherever you want to go?

  » Lights up.

- ME: So would you say you spend a good deal of time in other places besides here?

- ME: Or would you say you spend the majority of your time here?

  » Lights up.

- ME: I wonder why that is. Can you tell me your name?

- ME: I wonder—can you see us?

- SAM: Can you just hear us?
  » Lights up.

- ME: That's kind of weird. Did anybody ever hurt you when you were here?

- ME: Did you ever hurt anybody when you were here?

- ME: Do you remember?
  » Lights up.

- ME: One of the other things that I always wonder about, do you know what day it is? What year? Today is July 21, 2012. Did you know that?

- ME: Did you think it was a different time?

- ME: Does it matter anymore?
  » Lights up.

- ME: Don't let those people outside scare you off. I can hear them. I'm hoping they don't open the door. It's really loud.

- ME: Are you still with us?

- RANDOM GUY OUTSIDE THE DOOR TALKING: Is anybody in here?
  » Lights up.

- ME: That's funny! You've got a good sense of humor!

- ME: Just between us, do you think a lot of people running around here are stupid?

  » Lights up.

- ME: Me too. You know what else they are? Rude! [Video is interrupted by a group of people yelling out multiple strings of curses and ruining our session. They literally opened the door and came right on in and acted like we weren't even sitting in there with a video camera and flashlights out on the floor].

We thought it was hilarious when the flashlight was used to answer the intruder's question, "Is anybody in here?" We were absolutely cracking up over that. And even more so when he indicated that he thought the rude intruders were stupid!

Cell in New Wall

We walked all around this cell block and I found myself stopping in a random cell. We were able to capture another great flashlight session on video, and the excerpt is below:

- SAM: If someone just turned that light on, can they turn it back off so we'll know that's you?

  » Light turns off.

- SAM: Can you hear us?

  » Lights up.

- SAM: Thank you. All right, I'd like to ask you a couple of questions, can you turn it back off.

- SAM (to me): There's something about us, Jamie. Especially with all of this craziness going on.

- ME: Are you here because we called you here? Because we said we wanted to talk to somebody?

  » Lights up.

- ME: That's what I thought. The plot thickens. It keeps getting weirder and weirder.

- ME: Were you a prisoner here? Are you…

  » Lights up.

- ME: Just to confirm, I'll ask again. Just to make sure we heard you right. You were a prisoner here? Is that right?

  » Lights up.

- SAM: It might take him a little bit of time to turn on.

  » Lights up.

- ME: I've got one for you. A theory is that you're able to draw energy from that flashlight, but one of the things that I wonder about is, are you drawing energy from me, too?

  » Lights up.

- SAM: Jamie gets awful tired when she does these flashlight sessions. That might be one of the reasons why she gets so tired.

- ME: I knew it. I mean, I've been saying it. Okay, can you tell me—do you talk to a lot of people this way?

- ME: Is it just easier with us for some reason?

  » Lights up.

- ME: I don't know how I feel about that, but I think it's true—for whatever reason.

- ME: Do you think it's just easier somehow to talk to us? I think it's because we're trying to listen.

  » Lights up.

- ME: Are you still with us?

  » Lights up.

- ME: How about … did you ever love …

  » Lights up.

- ME: What I was going to ask you, a minute ago, was have you ever loved anybody?

  » Lights up.

- SAM: That was a pretty quick response.

- ME: I'll ask you a follow-up if you'll turn it back off. Let it go for me. Thank you. What I want to know about that— did it end well? Did you have a happy ending?

- ME: Do you think maybe that's partly why you're still here?

  » Lights up.

- ME: Do you know what happened to her?

  » Lights up.

- ME: Did she marry somebody else?

- ME: Did she die?

  » Lights up.

- ME: All right. I've got my follow-up, if you'll turn that light back down. I don't want to irritate you, but we are sitting in a prison. You told me that you were a prisoner here, that you loved somebody, and that it didn't end well. So, I think you know where I'm going here. Did you kill her? Don't get mad at me for asking, I mean look at where we are.

• ME: I'm not trying to make you mad, but I think it's a fair question. Do you at least agree with me that it's a fair question for our venue?

• ME: Did I piss you off? Like I said, I'm not trying to make you mad, I just kind of thought the conversation might have been headed that way. It's okay to tell us. I mean, whatever happened, we're not here to judge you or anything like that. We just want to know what happened.

• ME: Do you still want to talk?

• ME (to Sam): I think he killed her. I think that's exactly what happened. Don't you? Sam? I think he killed her.

• SAM: It's possible. He just went silent.

• ME (to Sam): Did you not just see how that played out? He said he loved somebody, it didn't end well, he knew what happened to her, she didn't marry somebody else, she died. And now he's gone because I nailed him. That's pretty screwed up.

• ME: Like I said. I'm not trying to piss you off. I'm not trying to do anything like that except just figure out what happened and if you know what happened and you can't talk about it…quite frankly, that's a problem. And I'm not talking about for me, I'm talking about for you. I know that for a fact. For you to know something to be true and for you not to be able to talk about it, I mean, quite frankly, that's bullshit.

I don't know what to say for myself after this session. This was really the only time that I have gotten rather combative and provoking. All that I can tell you is that I sensed I was talking to a murderer. This experience was completely opposite from the encounter I had at Mansfield. I was never scared. But I did completely lose respect for him since he wasn't able to face what he had done. Is it possible that I read this whole session wrong? Sure. Maybe he was innocent and got mad and left after I asked him if he killed the woman he was in love with. Maybe my imagination ran wild because of the environment. But that just wasn't the impression that I picked up on. My bullshit detector went off. Wrong or right, that's how I felt toward the end of this session, and that's how I left the session. We were going strong in the beginning of this session, and once I started really focusing in on some very real questions, I felt that the guy just couldn't handle it, so he stopped communicating with us. Usually, if you accuse someone who is innocent, they remain adamant and insist upon their innocence.

I later heard a story of Jeff Atkinson, an inmate who was murdered on this block by other inmates because he had killed a pregnant woman. I can't help but thinking maybe we somehow made contact with this guy.

Cafeteria—Last Session

Something about being in this kitchen was frightening to me. Maybe all of the old equipment still being around, as if the place just shut down yesterday, contributed to the eerie atmosphere. Or maybe something bad likes to hang around in there. A lot of many things bad, perhaps.

Excerpt from yet another flashlight video:

- ME: Do you know who the shadow man is?

  » Lights up.

- SAM: I have a little black box in my hand. And it's a recorder. It's got a little light at the top of it. Can you yell at the top of your voice the name of the shadow man.

- ME: Please turn it off because I want to ask you some more questions about this shadow man. Is it you? Are you the shadow man?

- ME: Is he in here too, though?

- ME: Are you still here?
  » Lights up.

- ME: I was just asking is the shadow man in here?

- SAM: Tell you what. Can you show yourself to us? Jamie was saying, two or three times today—that we might see something we haven't seen before. Now's the time. Jamie might have her eyes closed, but I'm looking.

For the record, I did not have my eyes closed. But we didn't see anything. Because of all the people walking around interrupting us, I was ready to go, and believe it or not, so was Sam. Again, of course this isn't West Virginia Pen's fault. You get what you get sometimes on a public hunt, and this is why serious hunters avoid public events. They will just get a group of their own people organized and shut the place down for the night. I wish that Sam and I had spent the money to shut the prison down just for the two of us so we could have ensured a quiet investigation. There is nothing like having a place to yourself.

The original prison structure. Inmates were
executed by hanging between 1899 and 1949.

The Wheel. I was captivated the moment I saw it. One of only two in existence—the other is in England—it separates the prison from the administration building, where the warden and his family lived.

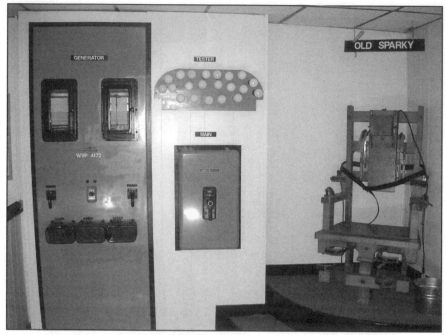

This is the real chair, not a replica like they have at the museum in the Mansfield, Ohio, reformatory. This chair saw nine executions from 1951–1959. West Virginia abolished the death penalty in 1965.

If You Decide to Visit:

Location & Contact Info

Moundsville Economic Development Council

818 Jefferson Ave.

Moundsville, WV 26041

Tel: 304-845-6200

Fax: 304-843-4146

Website

www.wvpentours.com

Type of Tours/Hunts Offered

Various historic tours offered; Public and private ghost events.

Haunted attraction for Halloween? Yes

Bathroom facilities? Yes

Safe room for sleeping/snacking? More of a break room.

Price: $60 per person for public hunts; $800 for private hunts—up to twenty people

Tips: Don't miss the day tour. You need it to learn the building, and the history deserves to be absorbed during the light of day.

Closest airports: Pittsburgh International Airport—48 miles away; Port Columbus International Airport—114 miles away; Cleveland Hopkins International Airport—118 miles away; and Washington Dulles International Airport—187 miles away.

Media Appearances

Ghost Hunters, Season 3, Episode 303—10/25/06

Ghost Adventures, Season 1—10/31/08

Ghost Lab—11/20/10

Paranormal Challenge—7/15/11

Paranormal State, Season 4, "Darkness Falls"

Stranded—Season 1, Episode 3—3/13/13

ABC's Scariest Places on Earth

Sam's Observations

West Virginia Penitentiary has a different feel to it than the other prisons that we investigated. Maybe it's because of all of the death that has occurred there. It's a foreboding place.

We had a few obstacles during the night, as a group of people who didn't know the etiquette of public ghost hunts kept running into us. It was a minor inconvenience, though.

Also, our IR camera went on the fritz when we first started trying to communicate in the psych ward. It just froze up as soon as we started to make contact. I had to take the battery out to get it to shut down! I was able to get it up and running as we continued with the session. It's never malfunctioned like that before or since. I can't explain it.

We did get some good evidence. A family on our day tour even caught a shadow person on video. That's the first time I've seen anything like that in the daytime!

TEN

MISSOURI STATE PENITENTIARY — JEFFERSON, MISSOURI

"The Walls" opened in March of 1836 and was finally closed in 2004. It was the oldest operating prison west of the Mississippi River. This place was around a full one hundred years before Alcatraz!

Some of the punishments utilized in the old days included:

- Whippings with a cat-o'-nine-tails
- The Water Cure—a dunking apparatus

- The Rings—A prisoner's hands were chained above his head, and he was forced to stand for hours, or in some extreme cases, for days on end.

- The Line—Prisoners were forced to stand at attention for eight hours or until they collapsed.

There was one major riot here in 1954 that resulted in four inmates being killed. There are 3,000 documented deaths, with countless unknown gravesites throughout the property. With 168 years of history and all of this death, it is very easy to see why this prison may have its share of hauntings.

Missouri State Penitentiary.

Our Experiences—August 25, 2012—
Day Tour and Public Investigation

We were lucky enough to take the day tour with a former deputy warden. He gave us an interesting and informative history of the prison. We heard accounts of old escape attempts and notorious prisoners such as Pretty Boy Floyd, Kate Richards O'Hare, and Emma Goldman, as well as stories of buildings that no longer stand and of what people tried to do to survive their time in the dungeon.

We were allowed to walk all through Housing Unit 4 and the gas chamber on the day tour. We did not see death row or the administration building during the day. The catwalks are still accessible and maintained in Unit 4. That was a uniquely Missouri Pen experience, to be able to walk across the open space to the other side of the cell block. It seemed to me to be a very dangerous thing to have, those catwalks. I asked about it, too: "Did anyone ever fall or get thrown off these catwalks?" I was told it never happened. The cells were considerably larger here than anywhere else we had been, although they sometimes held up to eight people at once. Another thing we noticed was that the cells were built to face each other, which we found out was done in the early days of prison design. By the time Mansfield and West Virginia Pen were built, prison systems had discontinued building cells that faced each other for security reasons.

There were only about twelve people on our public hunt, which was fantastic. For some reason, we were unable to capture any flashlight video during this investigation. We did, however, seem to capture plenty of EVPs. And we both had an amazing personal experience over on death row.

Administration Building

Female Housing Unit

We began the evening upstairs in the old female housing unit, which is above the administration building. What a weird experience to walk upstairs in this building and happen upon a full cell block! The size of it surprised us. Shortly before the prison closed, men were in this ward, and there is a notorious story of a man who was housed in Cell 85. The guards thought he was paranoid and delusional, but the prisoner was adamant that a female spirit was tormenting him at night, trying to get into his cell. The poor guy would sleep sitting up in his bed, curled into a ball. Cell 85 was the first place that Sam and I went to, and we believe that we were rewarded with an EVP. Here is our transcript:

- ME: Well, we're here on a kind of a public event tonight. But it's pretty small. There's only about twelve of us in the place. So we're hoping that fact won't, uh, deter anybody from coming to talk to us. We're in the (unexplained plastic cracking sound) female housing unit, so maybe uh …

- ME (to Sam): Sounded like somebody just cracked a plastic bottle.

- SAM: That's what I thought. It came from inside the room.

- ME: There ain't a plastic bottle.

- SAM: If anyone in the whole prison wants to come talk to us, you're welcome to.

- ME: Do we have any takers?

- SAM: Just going to be here a couple of more minutes.
  » UNKNOWN MALE: **Please, get out.**

We moved on to another cell and captured this:

- SAM: We've come all the way from Atlanta, Georgia, to visit with you guys.
  » K2 lights up.

- SAM: Can you do that again if that was you?
  » UNKNOWN FEMALE: **I'm dead.**

- SAM: If you need to take a minute, that's fine. We would like to see it light up again.
  » UNKNOWN FEMALE: Not good.

We had no idea that anyone was talking to us the whole time we were there! Neither one of us picked up on anything. A lot of times I will get a certain "feeling" about particular places within the buildings we go to. I might experience something more physical, such as the hairs standing up on my arms, or I may have more of an intuition that something feels a little "off." I could have been standing in line at Disney World for all I felt at that time (or didn't feel, rather). I could have been at the grocery store.

Basement with Tunnel Fenced Off

This is just a tiny little area underneath the administration building. Nothing much was going on down there, but it is worth a trek downstairs because of the neat-looking tunnel that is fenced off down there.

Offices in Administration Building

We had some seemingly random K2 hits in here. I was mostly just fascinated by the abandoned offices and was trying to figure out if that is really what dust looks like after a few years or if someone just spilled something all over the place.

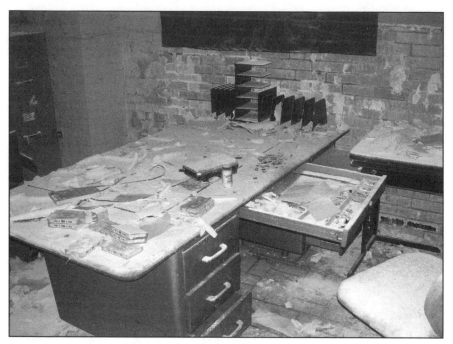

Old abandoned office in administration.

Housing Unit 3—Death Row

As soon as we went downstairs (below ground) to death row, which is underneath Housing Unit 3, I began to get excited. The place is downright eerie, and I fully expected something to happen to us down here. The photo on the bottom of page 183 doesn't accurately depict the mood. What you are looking at is the guard control box before you enter death row. The red lights are still glowing on the box, and all you see down there are just these spooky old red lights. It is the perfect horror movie setting. We've seen a lot of stuff this year, but when I happened upon this scene, it took me about thirty seconds to get my breath back. It just did something to me. The anticipation hit me full force.

The exterior of the death row section of the building.

The guard control cage outside of death row.
The red glowing lights cast a very eerie effect.

We shuffled on down the right side of the hallway and picked a cell to camp out in. I walked all the way in, and Sam was sort of standing outside in the hallway, quite a few feet away from me. I put the K2 down on the bed, and it immediately lit up to orange. I started talking, trying to get something to happen with the flashlights, but nothing was going on. I was having the same type of feeling that I had in the visitor's room in Mansfield—I just knew something was around us, and we just had to be patient and try to draw it out.

I kept on talking for several minutes. Suddenly, some movement occurred to the left side of Sam that caught my attention. I looked up and saw a big, burly shadow man standing right next to Sam (who is also 6-foot-2) looking in the cell at me! We were looking straight at each other. This wasn't something I saw out of the corner of my eye. This was something that appeared solid to me. He looked just like a person, except for a black mass, so I couldn't see his facial features or hair. He was just a shape of a man. My heart skipped a few beats. My brain fought to process what I was seeing. Everything was happening much too quickly. I said to Sam, "Something is standing right next to you!" Sam said, "You've got to be kidding me! I was just about to say something to you because I thought I was seeing something! You got it out before I could!"

I immediately turned on the flashlight I was holding (while talking to Sam) and pointed the light at the ground. I wasn't scared, but I was caught off guard—and certainly startled by what I saw. The sheer size of him was a bit ominous, but I wouldn't call him menacing. I was acting on pure instinct now.

I wish I wouldn't have said anything, because my sense was that he was coming in to interact with me using the flashlights. I didn't feel threatened by him at all. It was more just a "you called me here to talk, I'm here—what's going on?" He was just standing there checking us out. But I apparently acted like a complete amateur idiot and killed the mood, and he was gone. He didn't walk away or fade away. It was more like he just was standing there one second and then just wasn't anymore. The fact that we both experienced this simultaneously is just priceless to me. It makes it more real than anything I thought I saw by myself. When you have someone you fully trust telling you that they just had the same experience, you are a hundred times more willing to believe that it was real.

We tried another death row cell and caught the following EVP:

- ME: Anybody still down here? Can you come down here and let us know that you hear us…that you're still here?
  » UNKNOWN MALE: **I am.**

- SAM: Very excited to see you, if that was you. If you were doing the K2 earlier, can you try and turn on a flashlight for us, please?
  » UNKNOWN MALE: **Tough.**

At this point, our guides came down and got us because it was time to rotate buildings, so we had to end our session. When we left death row, we told our guides what we thought we saw. After we described the shadow man, they all nodded knowingly. He is a familiar figure to them. They have no idea who he is or what he is up to. But he is no stranger to death row.

Death row hallway, where the shadow man walked right up to us.

Housing Unit 4

It is hard to get any activity in an open area like this while you are on a public hunt. However, for a split second, I thought we were going to capture a flashlight video in a cell on the main floor. I was sitting there on the bed talking about how my very favorite thing is to watch the flashlight light up when one of them suddenly turned on. I said, "Okay, can you turn it back off for me?" The light went dark, and Sam turned the camera on. And all further activity ceased! I guess prisoners aren't known for being the most cooperative bunch of people.

On a catwalk, looking across to the other row of cells.

Inmate art on the walls inside a cell.

Dungeon in Basement of Housing Unit 4

If you are afraid of the dark, this is the place for you. The story goes that many men were driven insane down here. Or if they weren't driven insane, they emerged from the dungeon blind. Or a combination of the two. We heard the story of one former prisoner who had a button that he would throw on the ground and then spend all day looking for it so he would have something to focus on to keep him from going insane.

Nothing happened while the two of us were down there together, but Sam swears that after I left him alone, he felt something breathe on him. He also captured an EVP session while down there alone:

- SAM: Have a device in my hand, it's a recorder ... If you have anything to say, now is the time to say it. The best thing to do for us to know that somebody's here is to turn a flashlight on, or make that box there on the floor light up.
  » UNKNOWN MALE: **Get out!**

Gas Chamber

I know that this is a building where many souls met their deaths. But it didn't feel like anything to me. It just felt like another sterile, empty building. It could have been anything, anywhere, for how it made me feel (or rather, how it didn't make me feel). So these EVPs that we caught? Well, it just goes to show you that you never know what is going on beneath the surface! We were only in there about five or ten minutes, but we captured some amazing evidence on our recorder in that short amount of time.

The exterior of the gas chamber

• SAM: Just want to ask if there is anybody here with us, can you please turn on a flashlight … that we have laying on the floor?

» UNKNOWN MALE: **Run!**

» UNKNOWN FEMALE: They turn on gas.

What interests us about this particular EVP session is that Bonnie B. Heady was the only female ever executed in the gas chamber. It happened on December 18, 1953, and it was a dual execution alongside Carl Austin Hall. The two of them kidnapped and murdered a young boy named Bobby Greenlease. The family paid a $600,000 ransom (which at the time was the largest ransom ever paid in the United States), but Heady and Hall had already killed the child. Could we have captured their voices after all of this time? Are they still stuck here in the gas chamber, living out their deaths over and over again? Some would say that would be a well-deserved and fitting outcome for these two. The former deputy warden passed on a story from his predecessor to us, and Ms. Heady was called the coldest person at Missouri Pen. It is always shocking when a woman kills—especially when it is a child murder.

We even managed to capture some more evidence during our short stay in the chamber:

- SAM: Can you make the gray box light up?
  » UNKNOWN MALE: F_ _ _ you!

We were taken completely by surprise with the evidence we captured in the gas chamber.

We were pleasantly surprised by our visit and investigation at Missouri Pen. We never expected to see a shadow person standing straight in front of us on death row, and we certainly never expected to have possibly captured the voices of two of Missouri's most notorious murderers.

Inside the gas chamber.

If You Decide to Visit:

Location & Contact Info

Sheila Sanford, Tour Coordinator

115 Lafayette Street

Jefferson City, MO 65101

Tel: 573-632-2820

Website

www.missouripentours.com/msp.html

Type of Tours/Hunts Offered

Historic tours offered; Public and private ghost events.

Haunted attraction for Halloween?

Bathroom facilities? Port-a-potty

Safe room for sleeping/snacking? No

Tips: Don't worry if you forget to pack drinks for your hunt; the gift shop will be opened for the hunters, and you can buy water during the night.

Price: $95 for public hunts; $1,000 minimum for private events.

Closest airports: Columbus Regional Airport—17 miles away; Lambert-St. Louis International Airport—99 miles away; Kansas City International Airport—146 miles away.

Media Appearances

Ghost Hunters—11/2/11

Sam's Observations

A Shape Walks Among Us:

Jamie and I shared a great personal experience at Missouri State Penitentiary. We were down on death row doing a flashlight/EVP session. Jamie was inside the cell while I was standing just outside it, facing her. We hadn't had any luck with the K2 or with any of the flashlights going off in the cell. As we had done with previous prison cell sessions, if we don't get any responses, I'll step outside to give whomever we are trying to communicate with some room to enter. Being on the outside of the cell also allows me to observe the other cells on the block.

The area we were in wasn't pitch black, but it was fairly dark. I could see clearly about twenty-five to thirty feet on either side of me. While looking at the cells to my left, I suddenly saw the shape of a large, barrel-chested man walking toward me from about two cells down! Immediately, I thought that my eyes were playing tricks on me. There was no way I was seeing what I was seeing. When this shape got right up next to me, both of my legs got the chills. I wanted to say something to Jamie, but I kept thinking that this was some trick of the light.

Jamie suddenly stopped her line of questioning and said, "Something is standing right next to you!" I was stunned! Jamie verbally stated what I was thinking! There was really something standing next to me. The whole thing just blew my mind!

What a great investigation to end this book with!

CLOSING REMARKS

Looking back, I still don't know if I have any "special" abilities or sensitivities. I almost think what I have is an ability to listen. And to just talk to someone. Apparently, there are a lot of things out there that are willing to talk. I believe that I am an empath. I can feel the emotions of people, both living and dead. This would explain how I would be overcome with emotions that weren't mine in several locations, my ability to pick out places within the locations to try to conduct our sessions in, and how my energy is drained after our flashlight sessions. I can meet someone in death, just like in life, and see all the ways their hearts break.

Is it that these places themselves are haunted—or is it that they are serving as beacons for spirits? Because so many people are gathered in one place trying to communicate—is this what is bringing the "hauntings?" It seems that we encountered more travelers than spirits who are seemingly stuck in locations. In *Picture Yourself Ghost Hunting*, Christopher Balzano has come to the same conclusion. On page 23 he says: "As you get more involved, ghosts find you. They might hang around, waiting for their turn at the microphone, regardless of the location. Some people just draw in ghosts, but more often, people who do the work find odd things happen around them." I think we experienced that phenomenon. The ghosts or spirits found us when we called them out. We were convinced that this happened multiple times to us, that we made contact with someone because we wanted to talk and try to listen to them. It makes me want to conduct a series of investigations in locations that do not have any prior claims of paranormal activity and see what happens to us there. Is everywhere haunted? Are we haunted?

We will probably never know who or what it is that we are making contact with. For instance, I am always on high alert when I think we are speaking with a child. For some reason, I always think it is something bad trying to disguise itself as a child and draw us in. Of course, in life there really is no such thing as "always." But that's where my head takes it, and I am disturbed by spirits of children. Another possibility that I never considered until we went on our journey was that maybe all of these ghosts aren't dead people at all. Christopher Balzano touches on this idea briefly. What if what we are thinking is paranormal is just related to superstring theory or time slips? What if what we think are ghosts are actually real live people caught in between dimensions or alternate realities? Or not even caught— just people who are able to jump back and forth? What if Eugene Carter, who contacted us at Mansfield, isn't even dead? What if Eugene Carter is currently incarcerated somewhere and just figured out how to transport himself? I know, I know, I am talking crazy now. But maybe that's why the Ohio Department of Corrections didn't have a record on him. Who knows? Perhaps to me, this is one of the most fascinating things of all to think about.

What Else Have We Realized?

• Throughout all of our visits, we have never been disappointed in a boiler room or a basement.

• Our private sessions that have had multiple interruptions during public ghost hunts—including people walking in on us and walking around for a few minutes—did not drive the spirit away like we thought would happen.

• We are blown away by the sense of humor and intelligent interactions we experienced.

• We thought it was weird how some seemed to indicate that they could hear us but not see us.

• Some are lonely, but some are with others and interacting with them.

• It makes no difference whether it is day or night. You can experience something at any time.

Our preconceived notions changed in the sense that we realized there were no hard and fast rules for any of this. Some spirits seemed to be stuck (the suicides and prisoners spring to mind), and some indicated they were free to roam. Maybe when you die you don't immediately go elsewhere, or if you do, maybe you can go back and forth between heaven and earth. While it certainly seems logical to think that ghosts are either confused or fixated on some unfinished business or purpose, I don't think it is that simple anymore. We are all here on earth for a variety of reasons that are unique to our individual lives. And these reasons evolve as we grow into who we are—sometimes throughout our entire lives. What motivates and drives us changes. And I think maybe that could stay the same after we die. Our reasons are all different and in some cases, are always changing.

What do we get to take with us? I think our personality stays the same—we don't lose the essence of who we are. If we have a sense of humor, I think that stays. If we are playful or kind and nurturing, or whatever, I think it goes on. If we love and have love, I don't believe it disappears. And on that touchy-feely note, I also believe that if someone is a jerk in life, their behavior isn't going to be improved upon their death!

Our journey isn't over. We have many more places to explore, a lifetime of things to learn, and many more questions to ask. Where do these spirits go when they are not interacting with us? Are they lost somewhere, are they sleeping and resting in peace? Or are they sort of doing whatever it was they did in life still? Are they visiting museums, riding roller coasters, and still popping in to see their family? Maybe, in the end, we are all just travelers.

Sam and I wish you all well on your own ghost adventures. We hope that you will check in with us from time to time on our site, *www.americasbest ghosthunts.com.*

The last question I asked when I was sitting alone somewhere deep in the bowels of the Missouri Pen death row: Does dying hurt? And nobody answered me, of course. But I sat there in the dark, and I knew the answer anyway—no more than living does.

What terrifies me the most? Getting stuck out there in the great beyond alone and lost. But Sam told me: "Stay put. I will find you. Jamie, I will find you." I believe that he will.

Bibliography

"A Place in Time; Waverly Hills; Tuberculosis Hospital was Heart of an Isolated Community, Inspiring Loyalty in Patients, Staff in the First Half of this Century, the Waverly Hills Tuberculosis Sanitarium Gave a lot to the Neighborhood Below it." *Courier Journal,* November 23, 1989.

"State Hospital Gets Low Rating." *The Charleston Gazette,* April 6, 1985.

"Weston Patient Dies After Fight; Second Death Within A." *The Charleston Gazette,* September 29, 1992.

"Competency Tests Ordered For Patients." *The Charleston Gazette,* November 7, 1987.

Balzano, Christopher. *Picture Yourself Ghost Hunting.* Course Technology PTR, 2009. Distributed by Cengage Learning.

Belanger, Michelle. *The Ghost Hunter's Survival Guide: Protection Techniques for Encounters with the Paranormal.* Woodbury, MN: Llewellyn Publications, 2011.

Brake, Sherri. *Haunted History of the West Virginia Penitentiary: Afterlife with no Parole.* Raven Rock, 2011.

———*The Haunted History of the Ohio State Reformatory.* Charleston, SC: The History Press, 2010.

Brown, Alan. *Ghost Hunters of the South.* Jackson: The University Press of Mississippi, 2006.

Carr, Tom. *Talking to Yourself in the Dark.* Lulu.com. T&D Productions, 2010.

Clancy, Harrison. *Destination Frightville: 13 U.S. Haunts to Visit if you Dare.* 2012. Amazon Digital Services.

Clark, Bonnie. "Coles County Poor Farm: Local Resident Recalls Memories of Living There During Her Childhood." JG-TC.com. October 19, 2009.

Clemins, Jonathan D. *West Virginia Penitentiary.* Charleston, SC: Arcadia Publishing, 2010.

Egerton, Judith. "The Death Tunnel." *The Courier Journal,* May 15, 2004.

Hall, Christopher. "Waverly Hills Casts its Own Spooky Spell." *The Courier Journal,* October 29, 2003.

Hawes, Jason, and Grant Wilson. *Ghost Files.* New York: Gallery Books, 2011.

"Joe Bloxom Dead." *The Oakland Messenger* (Illinois), June 2, 1921.

Kleen, Michael. "From Poor House to Haunted House: The Coles County Poor Farm," *Historic Illinois* 34 (August 2011): 3-6.

———*Paranormal Illinois.* Atglen, PA: Schiffer Publishing Ltd., 2010.

———*Haunting Illinois. A Tourist's Guide to the Weird & Wild Places of the Prairie State.* Holt, MI: Thunder Bay Press, 2011.

Lageschulte, Melanie. "Old School Building in Farrar Offers Lessons in the Paranormal." *Des Moines Register,* October 18, 2010.

Leitch, Monty S. *In Appreciation of a Distinct Need.* Radford, VA: Commonwealth Press, 1991.

Mateo, Darhiana M. "Owners Saving Sanatorium." *The Courier Journal,* December 20, 2006.

Meyers, David, and Elise Meyers. *Central Ohio's Historic Prisons.* Charleston, SC: Arcadia Publishing, 2009.

Newman, Rich. *The Ghost Hunter's Field Guide.* Woodbury, MN: Llewellyn Publications, 2011.

Ontiveros, Roberto. "Group Set to Capitalize on Apparitions at Yorktown Hospital." *http://sacurrent.com* September 28, 2011.

Seventeenth Biennial Report of the Board of State Commissioners of Public Charities of the State of Illinois. Springfield, IL: Phillips Bros., 1902.

Smith, Scheri. "The Living Roam Waverly Hills." *The Courier Journal* September 26, 2005.

Smith, Stacy. "Discovering the Haunts of Ashmore Estates." *Daily Eastern News* (Illinois), October 19, 2007.

Starr, Patti. *Ghost Hunting Kentucky: America's Haunted Road Trip.* Cincinnati, OH: Clerisy Press, 2010. Distributed by Publishers Group West.

Taylor, Troy. *The Ghost Hunter's Guidebook.* Chicago: Whitechapel Press, 2010.

Wilson, Patty A. *Haunted West Virginia: Ghosts and Strange Phenomena of the Mountain State.* Mechanicsburg, PA: Stackpole Books, 2007.

Yorktown Historical Society and Nordheim Historical Museum Association. *Yorktown and Nordheim.* Charleston, SC: Arcadia Publishing, 2010.

Appendix A —
Tips We Picked Up

For Public Hunts

1. Always bring some Post-its and a pen. You can go in a room and close the door after you've put a sign up stating what time you entered and what time you will leave. If there isn't a door, bring a small traffic cone with you and set it up to block the entrance to let people know you are in the room. PEOPLE: if you see a traffic cone, please don't move it out of the way and come in the room anyway.

2. Never "hog" an area on a public hunt. Please rotate out and let everyone have a chance in the hotspots. Try not to stay longer than thirty to forty-five minutes in any area. This will help give everyone an opportunity to investigate.

3. Leave the most popular areas for later in the night—they always get crowded early in the evening. If you are serious, wait it out. Otherwise, people will walk in on you, or by the room, and make noise, and you will get very frustrated!

4. Don't bring Ouija boards.

5. Don't wear head lamps or bring very bright flashlights.

6. When using your flashlight, keep it pointed at the ground so you don't accidentally blind someone.

7. Everyone needs their own flashlight.

8. Don't run through the buildings, laughing and making a lot of noise.

9. Don't walk in on someone trying to do a session.

10. Do not wear flip-flops or any shoes that make noise, for that matter.

11. Do not leave your cell phone on!

12. And most certainly, DO NOT SHOW UP INTOXICATED!

In General

1. Essential items to have in your backpack: notebook, Post-it notes and pens, water, Kleenex, hand sanitizer, extra batteries for all your equipment, emergency snacks such as Sour Patch Kids or Haribo Peaches (if you are traveling with Jamie Davis), and peanut M&M's (if you are traveling with Sam Queen).

2. Don't whisper. It will mess up your EVP recordings. If you cough or make some other noise, say you did it so you don't get back home and think you caught something interesting like a ghost knocking on the wall.

3. If there are just two or three of you who want to get into a place for a private hunt but can't quite afford the price for it, contact the owner in the winter months when things are a little slower and ask if they will work with you on scheduling an event. You may be able to go on a Sunday night or during the week. Forget about October!

4. Utilize the safe rooms for all your eating and drinking. Respect the building and the owners. Treat every place like you would your own home. For some of you, treat every place better than you would your own home. Don't hide your trash throughout the buildings. Don't leave with anything that isn't yours, either. No taking "souvenirs" out of the building. This should go without saying.

5. Don't wait to try out your new equipment when you arrive at your ghost hunting location. Try out everything at home before you go to make sure you know what all of the buttons are for.

6. When possible, explore the location during the daytime so you can get acclimated to the building. If a day tour/historical tour is offered, make sure you take it. You will never regret this. This will also help you develop a game plan for the night, instead of walking around aimlessly.

7. During the tour, take notes. Jot down claims that correspond to certain areas. Also, be on the lookout for any interesting places that may not have had reported activity. Pay attention and note any rooms that you get any kind of feelings in or sense about.

8. Don't ask to be touched unless you are prepared to invite something to follow you home!

9. Don't run from anything, and don't show fear. We are also not fans of trying to provoke anything or anyone.

10. Clear your mind and concentrate. Listen to what your body is trying to tell you.

11. Be polite and courteous. Ask for what you want to happen; don't tell someone to do something.

12. Don't go alone. Nobody can make it alone.

Appendix B—
Basic Flashlight
Questions We Like to Ask

Flashlight Experiment

Introduce yourself and say you're here to talk with anyone who feels like helping you by answering some questions by playing with lights or talking into your recorder. Tell them how to work the flashlights by twisting the tops.

Line up three different colored flashlights in a row. See if you can get someone to light them up by the color you call out. Or, light them up all in a row—you don't care which one goes first.

For specific questions, tell them that lighting up means "yes." Give a good thirty seconds before moving on to the next question. Invite them to respond to the questions by speaking into the voice recorder as well.

Standard Questions for Flashlight Experiment

1. Are you male?

2. Are you female?

3. Are you a child?

4. Are you an adult?

5. Were you ever alive?

6. Is turning the light on hard for you? Does it take a lot of energy?

7. Are you always here at (name of place)? Are you always here in this room?
   (If nothing happens, ask them to speak into the recorder and tell you where they go when they're not here.)

8. Do you like it here?

9. Are you stuck here?

10. Are you unsure why you're here?

11. Have you tried to leave?

12. Are you here for a reason? (Ask them to tell you.)

13. Do you have friends here?

14. Do you have enemies here?

15. Is there anyone else with you right now? (Can go into how many, etc.)

16. Are you lost?

17. Did you die here?

18. Are you dead?

19. Do you believe in God?

20. Do you believe in heaven?

21. Do you believe in hell?

22. Are you in heaven?

23. Are you in hell?

24. Is it okay that we're here?

25. Do you get tired?

26. Do you miss eating?

27. Do you miss sleeping?

28. Do you get irritated with all these ghost hunters coming in here?

Appendix C—
Basic EVP Questions
We Like to Ask

EVP Sessions: Introduce yourself. State your purpose. Run a thirty-second delay before you ask another question.

1. Is there anyone here with us?

2. If there is, can you talk into this device?

3. If there is anyone who wants to talk with us, please say your name into our recorder.

4. Who all is in this building?

5. How many of you are there?

6. Can you tell me why I can't hear you right now? Can you knock or make some kind of noise so we'll know it's you?

7. Can you turn on one of these flashlights?

8. Can you manipulate the K2?

9. Can you tell us why you're here?

10. Are you dead?

11. How did you die?

12. Is this what you thought would happen when you died?

13. Do you like having visitors come in here and talk with you?

14. How old are you?

15. Do you like it here?

16. Can you manifest for us? Can you show yourself?

17. Do you know my name?

18. Is there anything you want us to know?

GET MORE AT LLEWELLYN.COM

Visit us online to browse hundreds of our books and decks, plus sign up to receive our e-newsletters and exclusive online offers.

- • Free tarot readings • Spell-a-Day • Moon phases
- • Recipes, spells, and tips • Blogs • Encyclopedia
- • Author interviews, articles, and upcoming events

GET SOCIAL WITH LLEWELLYN

Find us on

www.Facebook.com/LlewellynBooks

Follow us on

www.Twitter.com/LlewellynbookS

GET BOOKS AT LLEWELLYN

LLEWELLYN ORDERING INFORMATION

Order online: Visit our website at www.llewellyn.com to select your books and place an order on our secure server.

Order by phone:
- • Call toll free within the U.S. at 1-877-NEW-WRLD (1-877-639-9753)
- • Call toll free within Canada at 1-866-NEW-WRLD (1-866-639-9753)
- • We accept VISA, MasterCard, and American Express

Order by mail:
Send the full price of your order (MN residents add 6.875% sales tax) in U.S. funds, plus postage and handling to: Llewellyn Worldwide, 2143 Wooddale Drive, Woodbury, MN 55125-2989

POSTAGE AND HANDLING:

STANDARD: (U.S. & Canada)
(Please allow 12 business days)
$25.00 and under, add $4.00.
$25.01 and over, FREE SHIPPING.

INTERNATIONAL ORDERS (airmail only):
$16.00 for one book, plus $3.00 for each additional book.

Visit us online for more shipping options.
Prices subject to change.

FREE CATALOG!

To order, call
1-877-
NEW-WRLD
ext. 8236
or visit our
website

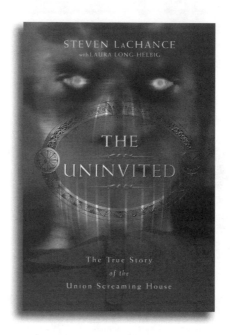

STEVEN LaCHANCE
with LAURA LONG-HELBIG

THE
UNINVITED

The True Story
of the
Union Screaming House

The Uninvited
The True Story of the Union Screaming House
STEVEN A. LACHANCE

Its screams still wake me from sleep. I see the faceless man standing in that basement washing away the blood from his naked body.

Steven LaChance was forever transformed by the paranormal attacks that drove him and his family from their home in Union, Missouri. When another family falls victim to the same dark entity, Steven returns to the dreaded house to offer aid and find healing.

Paranormal investigators, psychics, and priests are consulted, but no relief is found. The demon's presence—screams, growls, putrid odors, invisible shoves, bites, and other physical violations—only grows worse. LaChance chronicles how this supernatural predator infects those around it. But the one who suffers most is the current homeowner, Helen. When the entity takes possession and urges Helen toward murder and madness, LaChance must engage in a hair raising battle for her soul.

The Uninvited is a true and terrifying tale of extreme haunting, demon possession, and an epic struggle between good and evil.

978-0-7387-1357-1, 264 pp., 6 x 9   **$16.95**

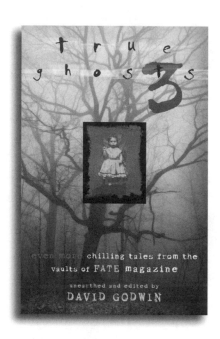

true ghosts 3

even more chilling tales from the
vaults of FATE magazine

unearthed and edited by
DAVID GODWIN

True Ghosts 3
Even More Chilling Tales from the Vaults of FATE Magazine
EDITED BY DAVID GODWIN

A spirit surgeon repairs a nurse's shattered arm. An Eskimo hunter provides for his family from the great beyond. The fearsome antics of a malevolent entity escalate to physical assault.

Documenting the strange, otherworldly, and truly bizarre since 1948, *FATE Magazine* offers another eye-opening collection of true stories that range from heartwarming to truly terrifying—encounters with departed family members and pets, protective angels and spirit guardians, ghost children, phantom vehicles, poltergeists, and vicious demonic beasts. Dating back to the early 1900s, these vivid eyewitness accounts—including out-of-body experiences, time slips, and dream visitations—offer an unforgettable and spine-tingling glimpse of the great unknown.

978-0-7387-2587-1, 336 pp., 5³⁄₁₆ x 8 $15.95

Marcus F. Griffin

Foreword by Jeff Belanger

EXTREME
PARANORMAL

INVESTIGATIONS

The Blood Farm Horror,
the Legend of Primrose Road,
and Other Disturbing Hauntings

Extreme Paranormal Investigations
The Blood Farm Horror, the Legend of Primrose Road, and Other Disturbing Hauntings
Marcus F. Griffin

Set foot inside the bone-chilling, dangerous, and sometimes downright terrifying world of extreme paranormal investigations. Join Marcus F. Griffin, Wiccan priest and founder of Witches in Search of the Paranormal (WISP), as he and his team explore the Midwest's most haunted properties. These investigations include the creepiest-of-the-creepy cases WISP has tackled over the years, many of them in locations that had never before been investigated. These true-case files include investigations of Okie Pinokie and the Demon Pillar Pigs, the Ghost Children of Munchkinland Cemetery, and the Legend of Primrose Road. Readers will also get an inside glimpse of previously inaccessible places, such as the former Jeffrey Dahmer property as WISP searches for the notorious serial killer's spirit, and the farm that belonged to Belle Gunness, America's first female serial killer and the perpetrator of the Blood Farm Horror.

978-0-7387-2697-7, 264 pp., 5³⁄₁₆ x 8   **$15.95**

The Ghost Hunter's Field Guide
Over 1,000 Haunted Places You Can Experience
RICH NEWMAN

Ghost hunting isn't just on television. More and more paranormal investigation groups are popping up across the nation. To get in on the action, you need to know where to go.

The Ghost Hunter's Field Guide features over 1,000 haunted places around the country in all fifty states. Visit battlefields, theaters, saloons, hotels, museums, resorts, parks, and other sites teeming with ghostly activity. Each location—haunted by the spirits of murderers, Civil War soldiers, plantation slaves, and others—is absolutely safe and accessible.

This indispensable reference guide features over 100 photos and offers valuable information for each location, including the tales behind the haunting and the kind of paranormal phenomena commonly experienced there: apparitions, shadow shapes, phantom aromas, telekinetic activity, and more.

978-0-7387-2088-3, 432 pp., 6 x 9   **$17.95**

Haunted Route 66
The Ghosts of America's Legendary Highway
RICHARD SOUTHALL

Pack the bags, hop in the car, and head west on a haunted journey of spine-tingling history and paranormal activity along legendary Route 66! This travel companion brings you from Chicago, Illinois, to Santa Monica, California, investigating over one hundred ghostly hot spots filled with fascinating facts and lingering spirits.

From amateur and professional ghost hunters to nostalgic fans, everyone can take their own haunted adventure on Route 66. Discover the famous highway through historic locations and gripping ghost stories about Al Capone and the gang wars of Chicago, Charlie Chaplin and the Venice Beach Boardwalk in Los Angeles, and many more. This one-of-a kind collection, with chapters organized by state, paves the way for your grand tour.

978-0-7387-2636-6, 240 pp., 6 x 9   **$15.99**

THE NIGHTMARE
ON BAXTER ROAD

ANATOMY *of a*
HAUNTING

LEE STRONG

Anatomy of a Haunting
The Nightmare on Baxter Road
Lee Strong

This is the true story of one couple's descent into darkness. In 1981, Jon and Carlie Summers moved into an inherited home in rural Iowa, leaving behind their workaday lives as a lawyer and a professor in Chicago. Soon after moving in, Jon and Carlie's lives begin a downward spiral as Carlie experiences violent dreams, possessions, hallucinations, and physical illness. Through old journals, nightmares, and personal encounters with evil, Carlie relives the history of the house, embodying its past of abuse, denial, obsession, broken lives, and death.

Anatomy of a Haunting is a terrifying true story that leaves Jon dead and pushes Carlie to the brink of insanity. Through interviews and exhaustive research into the 150-year old McPherson house, author Lee Strong delves into the history of the haunting and paints a nightmarish picture of one couple's descent into supernatural madness

978-0-7387-3552-8, 360 pp., 6 x 9   **$16.99**

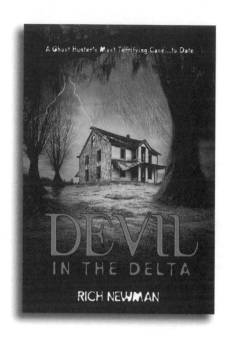

A Ghost Hunter's Most Terrifying Case...to Date

DEVIL
IN THE DELTA

RICH NEWMAN

Devil in the Delta
A Ghost Hunter's Most Terrifying Case... to Date
RICH NEWMAN

When author Rich Newman first arrives at the battered doublewide trailer deep in the Mississippi delta, it's clear that this is no ordinary haunting. Called from Memphis to assist a local ghost hunting team, Newman's investigation of the Martin house has become his most terrifying and mysterious case. What starts out as a malicious assault manifesting as deep rumbling sounds quickly spirals into a story of obsession, possession, witchcraft, and murder. When the evidence becomes overwhelming, long-buried memories from Newman's own past come back to haunt him—memories he'd rather forget. Collecting physical evidence, researching the violent history of the property, and sorting through the spiritual implications of demons, Newman's investigation of the Martin house is unlike any other.

978-0-7387-3516-0, 240 pp., 5³⁄₁₆ x 8   **$14.99**